<u>Dear David: Learning to See God through PTSD, Anxiety and Depression</u>
A Bible Study Book on David in 1 Samuel, 2 Samuel and the Psalms

Dear David: Learning to See God through PTSD, Anxiety and Depression
A Bible Study Book on David in 1 Samuel, 2 Samuel and the Psalms

By Genesis Pilgrim

Genesis Pilgrim
© 2019. All rights reserved.
ISBN: 978-1-7333145-0-3
www.genesispilgrim.com

To David,
Rest, dear friend, until the Day when you arise to receive your allotted
inheritance.

Contents

About the Cover Art

The cover art masterfully captures the message of this book. Indeed, the reader could understand the entire book just by a thorough examination of the cover picture. In tribute to this terrific piece, I would like to share some of my reflections . . .

The colors are sketchy throughout, often bleeding beyond the clear black borders that attempt to "contain" them. Thus we find the human experience. Try as we might, clearly capturing anything is near impossible as the mind allows different experiences to blend into one another.

In the art, the weapons are red. Signifying the past trauma of the warrior, these weapons send forth threads directly into the heart of the warrior, David—thereby showing his past always attempts to pull at the core of his being.

The colors of God in this art are the various shades of blue and white. In similar fashion to the red threads of the weapons, the supernatural is likewise sending forth threads into the heart of David. This signifies the inner conflict of the warrior as he struggles to reconcile past with present in his desire to spiritually transform beyond the negative experiences that have long held captive his heart.

David is purple—the color of royalty, and the result of mixing red and blue. Thus, God formed this great king through a combination of both the red of trauma and the blue of supernatural. This is encouraging. Although trauma may affect the person, somehow those past horrors can be used in positive transformation.

The bearded David carries on his back a bright red bow—which shows although he is in the midst of spiritual transformation, he is still a powerful warrior ready to defend his nation. The bow is a distance weapon, which represents the warfare activities of a king who directs generals but seldom participates in hand to hand combat. Thus, although David set behind him his sword and shield, he ever maintains his bow.

Within the brain of David, the red and blue combine into a light purple—showing his brain is attempting to make both colors (red, blue) into

i

a fully integrated picture of self (purple). Nonetheless, bright red holds captive the forefront of David's brain—signifying how the person with PTSD is more readily governed by his adaptations to past experiences.

However, the real "conflict" for the spiritual warrior takes place within the heart, not the brain. Although the brain may develop PTSD as "natural" coping mechanisms, the heart can provide a direct link to the supernatural. Within the heart of David, the red and the blue interact with one another. The white lines extending off the heart signify something magnificent is happening as these threads meet in the heart.

The bright light of supernatural activity in the heart is causing blue and white to radiate outward—reflecting on the red shield behind David. This signifies that, although the trauma of the warrior is behind him in his past, God is fighting to even transform those past events. God's light is fighting to reclaim the weapons that have been marred by past events.

In the art, ironically, David is oblivious to his own heart and shield transformation because he is turned away from them. David's limited vision does not allow him to fully perceive what is happening within him.

The hand of David is upturned, with his gaze being directed to the intersection of his forefinger and thumb. Perhaps he is grasping something small—maybe even a hair that is hanging from his head. This aspect is obscured to the observer—showing that the mind of the warrior is elusive to the observer as they are in the midst of an ultimately solo journey of discovery assisted by God. The obscuring of the left arm further illustrates this.

Moreover, David's attention is fixed on the relative inactivity of his thumb and forefinger, while within his heart occurs an explosion of brilliant light—which is even transforming the colors of the weapons behind him. Thus the warrior may ever remain stuck focusing on the wrong things— being oriented away from those true activities of dramatic positive transformation.

The observer is in a position to speak encouragement to David: *"Look at the miracle that is happening within your heart!"* . . . or . . . *"Look at how far you have come since that past experience."* However, without an observer to redirect his gaze, it is unlikely David will ever see the full miracle that is happening within his own heart. Therefore, this art speaks directly to observers. It beckons observers to assist warriors and those who suffer from trauma by speaking encouragement—positively redirecting the gaze of those who suffer.

There is much to ponder within this picture—offering us an artistic rendering of trauma, survival and faith. I hope it will provide encouragement to you as you read. Think often of the red, blue and purple. Faith is about survival. In that process, we all have a part to play. All observers are beckoned to speak encouragement to those who suffer— encouraging them to see the miracles occurring within.

Survive.

Help others to survive.

How to Use this Book

Bible Study Guide

This book is intended to serve as a Bible study book. When reading you will want to have a Bible near you. Then you can look up the Bible passages mentioned and develop your own thoughts. Feel free to jot down your own notes—determining whether you agree or disagree with my points. Overall, I want to assist people in "decoding" and making sense of these Bible passages.

This book discusses the 26 Traumatic Experiences of David, interpreting each experience through modern psychology. If you are interested in Bible study, this book will provide helpful notes on 1 Samuel, 2 Samuel and the Psalms of David.

If you are reading this book as a guide to the various Psalms of David or specific passages in the Bible, please feel free to use Index #1 in this book for quick reference.

David Character Study

If you are interested in psychology and how it merges with spirituality, this book will provide an analysis of David's traumatic experiences and how they affected him. The goal of this book is to psychologically analyze David through the psalms he wrote.

If you are interested in this topic, I recommend reading through each section of this book.

Limited in Time?

If your time is limited, skip ahead and read "Section 4." In this section I summarize Sections 1-3 of the book. Then if you would like to see how I arrived at those conclusions, you can go back to read the earlier sections of the book.

Introduction

David

Perhaps we know more about David than any other person in the Bible. In addition to the many details offered on events in his life in the books of Samuel, Chronicles and 1 Kings, we have many psalms David wrote himself. This gives us tremendous insight into the events which shaped David, and how he psychologically processed his traumatic experiences.

David was instrumental in the development of Christian spirituality. About half the Psalms were written by David. Many of these psalms were quoted in the New Testament—which means that understanding the mind, heart and spirit of David is central to our own relationships with God.

Considering the "whole person" of David, and his potential psychological disabilities from a lifetime of battles, we are able to unlock the intense emotions that drive many of his psalms.

As we venture to understand how the traumatic experiences shaped David's worldview, we develop a deeper understanding of human nature. Trauma changes people. By viewing David through the lens of his trauma, we can build a stronger appreciation for him as a historical person. Moreover, by understanding the unbearable trauma he endured, we get a fuller picture of the power of his faith.

David's faith was indeed powerful. His faith enabled him to survive numerous battlefields, betrayals, threats and plots. Indeed, if we welcome David as a faithful man ever standing strong in the midst of tragedy, we can likewise gain a faith which allows us to "survive" at all costs. Faith is about survival. David teaches us a faith which is remarkably personal—where God interacts with everything around us to protect us.

Post-Traumatic Stress Disorder (PTSD)

Post-traumatic stress disorder (PTSD) is a disorder developed by traumatic experiences—such as combat, physical injury and other tragedies. PTSD affects a person by causing them to have reactions to their surroundings that do not fit the situation. To protect the body, the brain gives the person a rush of adrenaline, tunnel vision and a flood of other effects to prepare them to react to a perceived dangerous situation.

A person with PTSD may experience random sequences of these effects throughout their daily routines. Some of the PTSD symptoms can be very intense, even causing heart beat pattern disorders like atrial fibrillation. (*In Section 2 of this book, the PTSD symptoms of David will be discussed in detail.*)

Throughout each chapter we will interact with different effects of PTSD that affected David during his many combat experiences and trauma. Although PTSD is a disabling effect of war, this book will show how PTSD is an essential part of Bible faith as it exists today. The combat experiences of David heightened his awareness of the unseen—allowing him to perceive God in ways others cannot. (*My conclusion is found in Sections 3-4 of this book, where I provide notes demonstrating how David's PTSD permanently transformed Bible faith through derealization and depersonalization.*)

In the Bible it is said, "we live by faith, not by sight" (2 Cor. 5:7). The development of Christian spirituality is centered on the ability to perceive spiritual things. A person who lives by faith is governed by a physically unseen reality. Where do we get this concept of faith? In this book I will show faith is a coping tool which can develop within those who survive trauma. So whereas the effects of PTSD can be disabling; the same effects of combat PTSD can form the basis of a person's faith in God.

If the PTSD mind naturally imagines danger, then it is natural for that same mind to develop the ability to perceive safety in God. This is exactly what we see in the Psalms of David. Although David experienced danger, he developed the ability to spiritually perceive God as rescuing him from those dangers.

Throughout the Bible, the Holy Spirit continues to invite people to interact with God using this same "PTSD-type" mechanism. Rather than imagining the negative, we are encouraged to imagine the positive reality of God's presence with us. Thus, Bible faith involves learning how to turn the imaginations of the PTSD mind into a supernatural reality that can be "seen" by the heart.

For the person afflicted with PTSD, the "imaginations" of the mind are "real." A panic attack forces our heartbeat and breathing patterns to change. A panic attack causes our focus to change completely. Thus the PTSD mind can also be used to create a positive spiritual reality that is just as "real."

This is exactly what David did. The pattern of Bible faith expects us to do the same. We are called to look at all situations with spiritual vision— seeing what we cannot with our physical eyes. Ultimately faith is the result of trauma. Christian faith is the result of coping with trauma through spiritual vision. In the midst of traumatic experiences, David "sees" God.

If you desire this powerful faith, read further. Take notes. Pray and allow the ancient words of David to instruct you on how to survive. Teach your mind to "see" the supernatural fortress of God that can protect you in the midst of all battlefields.

Book Structure & Topics

The purpose of this book is to examine how David's relationship with God was deepened through traumatic experiences. If David did not have these bad experiences he likely would not have developed into a man of such strong faith. In this way, faith is the direct result of dealing with tragedy. As a person encounters tough situations they are able to make the decision to shift their focus upon God.

This book will examine the many tragedies experienced by David. Section 1 of this book will examine the 26 Traumatic Experiences of David. We will discuss how he coped with each tragedy.

Then at the end of each "Traumatic Experience," I will present a "Dear David" letter. The purpose of each "Dear David" letter is to speak directly to David within his experience—speaking to him as a coach, counselor and friend.

This book should provide encouragement to all of us who have experienced trauma. By reflecting on the experiences and mind of David, and addressing him in each situation, we can find encouragement for our own struggles. The hope is that every reader will put themselves in the position of David. Allow each "Dear David" letter to speak encouragement in your own life.

The goal is that each of us will embrace the bad situations of life—allowing ourselves to find spiritual growth in the midst of each struggle.

Three Types of Davidic Psalms: Experience Psalms, Symptom Psalms & Seeing Psalms

I have always been intrigued by the sharp emotional swings present in David's psalms. When reading his psalms, we see David could rapidly alternate between very positive and negative thoughts instantly. We get the impression that his mind would race through conflicting thoughts. So, in my book, I make sense of these strong emotional shifts. I do this by matching his psalms with certain experiences in David's life. I also do this by matching certain observations to common PTSD symptoms experienced by warriors like David.

In my writing below I did my best to provide a classification system that would make sense of the emotional differences in David's psalms. I simplified all of his psalms into three types: Experience, Symptom and Seeing.

The "Experience Psalms" contain elements I think can be convincingly traced to traumatic experiences described in the books of Samuel; whereas the "Symptom Psalms" do not contain elements that can be convincingly traced to specific situations. Last, the "Seeing Psalms" are the psalms that were intended by David to teach future generations to "see"

God. Therefore, the Seeing Psalms do not contain many of the PTSD symptoms, with the exception of derealization and depersonalization.

Experience Psalms are psalms in which David reveals details that can be linked to specific traumatic experiences in his life. Throughout the "Traumatic Experiences 1-26" of Section 1, we will discuss the various Experience Psalms that provide helpful information. This will enhance our understanding of the historic events of 1 & 2 Samuel. The Experience Psalms include Psalm 2-4, 7, 9, 17, 18, 20-23, 25-27, 30-32, 34, 35, 38, 40, 41, 51, 52, 54-61, 63, 69, 86, 101, 108, 124, 138, 139 and 142-144.

Symptom Psalms are psalms in which David "vents" to the Lord. Unlike "Experience Psalms," Symptom Psalms do not contain clear details that allow us to narrow them down to a specific event in David's life. However, Symptom Psalms are useful in showing us the thought patterns of David—including how he viewed God, himself and others. In Section 2 of my book we will examine the Symptom Psalms of David by discussing the PTSD symptoms revealed in each. The Symptom Psalms include Psalm 5, 6, 8, 11-14, 16, 19, 28, 36, 37, 39, 53, 62, 64, 68, 109, 110, 140 and 141.

Seeing Psalms, where David's writing focuses on influencing future generations to "see" God, were likely written within the period in David's life before and after the transportation of the ark to Jerusalem. These psalms focus on providing teaching while excluding many of the PTSD symptoms that characterize David's other psalms. The only PTSD symptoms found throughout these psalms are depersonalization and derealization. During this stage, David was focused on serving as a liturgical leader of Israel, so these Seeing Psalms are focused on the exclusive goal of helping people to "see" God for themselves. As such, the two PTSD symptoms of depersonalization and derealization were intended to be carried forth as part of Biblical faith. Future Bible believers learn to "see" God through derealization and depersonalization. The Seeing Psalms will be discussed in Section 3 of my book. The Seeing Psalms include Psalm 15, 24, 29, 65, 70, 72, 95, 103, 122, 131, 133 and 145.

My classification system shows David originally experienced certain emotions that are linked to traumatic experiences (Experience Psalms).

Then after David survived those traumatic experiences, his mind continued to be afflicted with PTSD symptoms (Symptom Psalms). Last, David filters out all of the negativity, and intends to pass on the "positive" faith effects of derealization and depersonalization to future generations (Seeing Psalms). This allows future believers to also "see" God.

Within this classification system, there are some psalms that could be classified as one type or another depending on the author's thoughts on details within each psalm. In some cases, I determined a psalm did not contain "convincing" enough evidence for me to assign it to a traumatic experience from 1 Samuel or 2 Samuel. In other cases you may think I went too far in assigning a certain psalm to a traumatic experience because you are not convinced by the details therein.

However, I think my classification system is sufficient in its purpose—demonstrating that David experienced PTSD that is linked to situations in his life, and that after he mentally processed those emotions, he made an intentional effort to pass on derealization and depersonalization to future generations to teach them to "see" God.

(For a detailed discussion of PTSD symptoms experienced by David, feel free to use Section 2 of this book. In Section 2, a list of PTSD symptoms are provided along with page references detailing where David exhibits each PTSD symptom in the Bible.)

Disclaimer: This book is not intended to diagnose readers with PTSD. If you, or anyone you know, is struggling with trauma, seek the advice of a licensed counselor. A licensed counselor can properly evaluate psychological disorders and provide a treatment plan, including cognitive processing therapy (CPT), to help you on the road to recovery.

Section 1: David's Traumatic Experiences & the Experience Psalms

(Psalm 2-4, 7, 9, 17, 18, 20-23, 25-27, 30-32, 34, 35, 38, 40, 41, 51, 52, 54-61, 63, 69, 86, 101, 108, 124, 138, 139, 142-144)

Experience Psalms are psalms in which David reveals details that can be linked to specific traumatic experiences in his life. Throughout the discussions of "Traumatic Experience 1-26" this section, we will examine the various Experience Psalms that enhance our understanding of the historic events of 1 & 2 Samuel.

Before reading about each "Traumatic Experience," familiarize yourself with the Bible passages listed below each title. To help, I include a line after each "Traumatic Experience" title that lists the Bible passages discussed. Look for the double-star (**) to see the passages you "should" read. All other Bible passages are provided only as "optional" references.**

Traumatic Experience 1: <u>Kills Lion and Bear</u>

Read 1 Samuel 17:34-37 & Psalms 22, 27

The setting of this story is that the boy, David, goes into the army camp and is considering fighting against the giant, Goliath, to rescue Israel. In this story, David approaches King Saul and volunteers for this fight. "Champion Warfare" was common in the ancient world. Rather than two kings potentially losing an entire army of soldiers, each king would pick their best fighter and they would fight. Then the armies would interpret the outcome of that champion battle as the will of the gods. To rescue the entire army of Israel, David volunteered to be the champion.

King Saul rejected David—saying he lacked experience. However David goes on to explain he killed both a lion and a bear. The passage says David struck the predator to rescue a sheep, then the animal turned on him. David said he killed both the lion and the bear after seizing them by their hair. This means David did not kill the lion and bear from a distance, but he was in close, physical contact with them. This is a noteworthy accomplishment and is especially relevant.

David explains that since God delivered him from getting swiped with the paw of the lion and the paw of the bear, then God would also deliver him from getting hit with the weapon of Goliath. Perhaps the prospect of meeting Goliath in battle could be a flashback trigger of when he faced the lion and the bear. Thus, it would make sense that David would mention these to Saul.

At this point we may be inclined to just stand in awe of David's faith and physical strength. He had such an amazing faith in God. His complete trust in God is inspiring. It is exceptional that David had the courage to chase down a lion and a bear.

But is there more to this account? When considering the life of David, we must examine the young boy who was put in these especially traumatic situations.

Can we imagine what it would be like to be a young boy, alone in the wilderness with a flock of sheep? In John 10, the Lord Jesus tells us shepherds would know their sheep by name. The sheep could even recognize the voice of their own shepherd. When a stranger spoke the sheep could discern it was not their own shepherd. This is sufficient to show us shepherds cared for their sheep, and sheep cared for their shepherd. Shepherds would care for their sheep, providing protection during the long hours of the day and night, and in return the sheep would provide wool.

We can imagine David as a young shepherd boy. He would have been emotionally connected to his sheep. It would have been terrifying for David to see a predator attack one of his friends.

Today we might have a similar flood of emotions within us if we were to see our family dog or cat attacked by a predator. That flood of emotions would likely inspire us to do anything we could to rescue our "friend" from danger. We may be so compelled by adrenaline we would throw off any common sense—chasing down a bear with fists clenched and fire in our eyes to answer the cries from the one we loved.

However, this situation happened to David—not once, but twice. The first time it happened would have been very traumatic for the boy—forcing him to make a snap decision, without a moment to spare. After rescuing the first sheep however, David's parents continued to allow the boy to go out alone with the sheep.

If your son were in a similar situation, and told you about it, what would you do? If your son told you a bear came into your backyard, grabbed your dog and carried it off, then he chased the bear and killed it with a stick, what would you do?

If I were the parent in this situation, I would build a fence to keep out predators, then I would get a rifle so my son would be able to kill a predator from a distance. But would I continue to allow my son to do the same thing that led to the first tragedy?

As we can imagine, David narrowly escaped with his life in the first situation with the lion. If David would have tripped or dropped his weapon, the lion could have easily overcome David. However, after this close call, it appears the parents of David continued to send out their boy—alone and improperly armed, with the sheep. This leads to the unlikely occasion for the same situation to occur again. In this case lightning strikes twice. David has another predator carry off a sheep and he has to kill it while being close enough to grab its hair.

Later in life we can see David's relationship with his father and mother were damaged by these situations. In Psalm 27:10, David mentions that his parents rejected him. In Psalm 22:10, David says he was cast upon God from the moment he came from his mother's womb. A similar passage is found in Psalm 69:8.

When someone has survived tragedy, their mind develops coping strategies to protect them from harm. In this case, the fact that David's parents allowed him to be put at risk multiple times solidified his mind's distrust of his parents. Therefore in David's mind he was indeed a boy who was rejected by his parents, and cast upon the Lord from the moment of birth—left alone in the wilderness to care for himself and his sheep. Later in David's life it is no coincidence his parent's family is seldom seen beyond a brief stay in Moab and the appearance of several nephews in his army and court.

David's name means "loved." Yet at the critical points in his life mentioned above his parents did not demonstrate "love" for him. They did not invite him to meet the prophet Samuel. His parents did not protect him from lions and bears. Moreover, his parents allowed him to be thrust within warfare—beginning with Goliath and extending for the rest of his remaining childhood. It is likely David's name ("loved") served to bring these suffering contradictions to mind during his many sleepless evenings in the wilderness. Thus, the name of David—although meant for good, was twisted by repeated trauma into a reminder of how he "was not loved."

As we finish our discussion of this tragedy of David, let's summarize the mind of the boy who faced down the lion and the bear. . . . (1) It would be traumatic for a boy to hear the cries of a pet being killed. (2) It would be traumatic for a boy to have to kill a large predator, being close enough to grab it by its hair. (3) It would be traumatic for the boy to continue to be sent out by his parents into danger being improperly equipped. (4) It would be traumatic to have the same type of situation happen twice, leading to a doubling of all the trauma listed above—especially when we consider David's father still continued to send him out alone after the second attack.

Moreover, the accounts of the predators seem jumbled into the same description. It could be David was trying to simplify the two predator accounts in his discussion with King Saul. It could also be these predator attacks were so significant for the boy David his mind experiences an inability to recall key features of each event. So within the mind of David, the two attacks are linked in his memory by a similar sensation of fear and adrenaline. In PTSD, this is a common symptom. The mind of a person can cause traumatic events to become fragmented due to the shift that occurs in the brain as it poises the body to fight through a traumatic event. In other words, the person sees red as they jump into a traumatic situation, and after the situation is resolved the events are remembered only as a blur of actions.

Does our heart break for the boy David? We long to hear of someone who encouraged David as a child. But ultimately he was treated as an errand runner by his father and as a hired hand sent off with sheep into dangerous situations. Within this trauma however, God emerges as the source of strength for David. When he could rely on no one else, and while even his own relatives rejected him, God grants David "spiritual vision" to see the unseen. God brings him through these situations to give him faith to rescue his entire nation from the hand of Goliath. So God used all things for good.

If there had not been a crying sheep, David would not have had a heart for the army of Israel. If there had not been a lion and a bear, David would not have had the courage to stand before Goliath. And if David's relationship with his earthly father were perfect, he would not have felt the desire for a heavenly Father. Trauma brings opportunities for faith.

Dear David,

You are so brave and strong! I cannot imagine the courage it took for you to chase down the lion and the bear. I can tell you love your sheep. There are so many in this world who do not care for anyone beyond themselves. Often we can tell so much about a person by the way they treat their animals. An animal is not able to truly pay us back for our kindness to them, so when we are merciful and kind to an animal it shows we are doing this out of a simple heartfelt mercy without expecting repayment. This is exactly what you did when you rescued your sheep.

The courage and mercy you showed in rescuing your sheep shows the quality of your heart. You will grow into a man who has mercy for those in the world who can never repay your kindness. You will go on to extend mercy to the crippled and outcast, bringing those into your fold which have been rejected by society. You will make much of the wounded, rescuing them from despair and putting them back upon the path of salvation. How you treat your sheep is how you will treat your people. God sees your kindness extended to those sheep who cannot repay, and God will repay your kindness on their behalf.

I am saddened to hear about your relationship with your parents. All parents love their children. At times we do not do a good job expressing it. We are all a mess in one way or another. Sometimes parents have so much stress put on them they lose sight of the things that really matter. The most important thing in this world is to be there for our children, because in the end they are the only part of us that lives on. I am so sad to hear you feel forsaken being sent off into the wilderness with your sheep. There are so many people who feel this same type of rejection. But we can help one another. If you need a brother, I will be your brother.

I understand how you feel. You feel alone, as if from the very moment you were born you were rejected and cast upon God. This is a tough thing, but eventually we all get to a place where we realize we have to rely on God. It is never good to cope with rejection from family or people, but if this helps us to grow closer to God, then we are making progress.

7

We need to learn to rely on God and to surround ourselves with people who support us. If your family does not provide this type of support to you, I know countless people who would want you as a friend! You are courageous, brave, merciful and willing to put your life on the line for those you love. Anyone would be blessed to have you as a friend! Please be encouraged! I look forward to speaking with you in the future. If you would like my help with watching over the sheep, please let me know.

Sincerely,

Genesis Pilgrim

Traumatic Experience 2: <u>Champion Battle with Goliath</u>

Read 1 Samuel 17:38-57 & Psalm 138

In this story, the Philistine giant, Goliath, is challenging Israel's army. Rather than King Saul risking the loss of his entire army, he is considering sending out one soldier to fight Goliath. Realizing that no one is willing to serve as King Saul's champion, David volunteers.

When considering the background of David leading up to this point, the theme of being "despised" was a constant for David . . .

First, David was despised by his parents. When the prophet Samuel arrived at their home, all the sons were invited except for David. As the meeting continued, David was not mentioned until the prophet asked if the parents had any more sons. Then they said David was with the sheep. This shows David was treated similar to a household servant.

Second, David was despised by his brother, Eliab. David was sent on an errand by his father. When David arrived in the army camp, he began speaking to some of the soldiers. When David's brother heard him, he insulted David. He pejoratively asks where David left the sheep, which strikes as an insult—as if to say David had no purpose beyond watching the flock.

Third, David was despised by King Saul. When David courageously volunteered to fight the giant Goliath, King Saul despised David. He told David he was only an inexperienced boy who could not fight. In this way, King Saul wrongly judged David on his appearance—being unfamiliar with the fiery, courageous heart of faith within David.

Last, David was despised by Goliath. As David approached his adversary, Goliath referred to him as a stick before a dog—which was most likely due to David's lack of armor and traditional weapons, such as a sword or spear. The young David, with a slingshot in hand, was derided by Goliath.

Due to David's traumatic experiences with the lion and the bear, he would have been especially vulnerable to "rejection" from people. We

9

noted previously David felt rejected by his parents from moment he was born. So leading up to this experience before Goliath, there were several instances that cut at the heart of David's previous trauma. He was rejected and send away from his parents. Now as he tried to find his place in society, he received wave after wave of rejection from others—even the King himself made fun of David. Then the strongest warrior on the battlefield, Goliath, made fun of David.

The mind affected by PTSD has a way of tunnel visioning onto areas of perceived vulnerability. Because his parents' rejection led to David being in danger in two similar situations with a lion and a bear, the public rejection of David by his brother, Saul and Goliath would have cut on this previous wound of vulnerability.

He was already rejected by his parents—now it seemed the entire world was also rejecting David. So under this pressure of repeated rejection, what would David do?

Rather than buckling under insults, David used them as opportunities to show his great faith in the Lord God Almighty. Goliath insulted David. Then David trusted in the Lord God, saying the battle belongs to Him.

In this case it appears the challenge of this battle was not the fighting. In the Psalms David does not mention any difficulty in fighting itself. He was proficient in military skill. David's real challenge involved overcoming waves of rejection. Later in the Psalms, David frequently mentions his difficulties with criticism and rejection. Perhaps the rejection experiences leading up to his fight with Goliath are the source of his frequent relationship problems later in life.

So although David was a proficient, powerful warrior, he consistently struggled in his relationships with family and others. His early experiences of rejection found here in this passage stick with him for his entire life—serving to spread negativity throughout all his future experiences. David's life becomes a repeating pattern where he must always choose to divert his attention from the criticisms of others. He becomes so sensitive to criticism he imagines others are criticizing him in secret. The critical comments and negative treatment of David, received from his parents, brother, King Saul and Goliath, continue to swirl in his battle-scarred mind, resulting in David always imagining people plotting and whispering against him.

As David prepares and enters onto the battlefield, he exhibits risky behavior. Breaking with the tradition of the army, David rejects the use of any standard military equipment. Then the fire within David burns as he trades words across the battlefield with his opponent. He does not walk toward the giant. The young David runs (1 Sam. 17:48).

Psalm 138 *may* have been written to commemorate David's battle with Goliath. The details of this psalm line up well with the situation faced by David in this Bible passage. Goliath curses David by his "gods," then David offers praise to the Lord in the presence of this cursing (1 Sam. 17:43-45 & Psa. 138:1). The reference to the temple in Psalm 138:2 could be referring to the house of the Lord where Samuel ministered. At this early stage in his life, the shepherd David views himself with great humility—describing himself as lowly (Psa. 138:6). Goliath despised David, looking down upon him in anger (1 Sam. 17:42 & Psa. 138:7). Nevertheless, David stepped into the conflict—trusting the Lord to deliver him from trouble (1 Sam. 17:37 & Psa. 138:7).

In the aftermath of the champion battle, it is likely David lost respect for his brother Eliab—further lending to his social impairment. Just as it was the responsibility of David's parents to provide reasonable security for David, so also it was the responsibility of Eliab to provide reasonable concern for his younger brother. Instead, Eliab insults David and does not object to him stepping into the fray. In the future, it is likely these failures within David's family contributed greatly to his feelings of isolation. As a boy, David developed the abiding sentiment that his family did not care about him. This stuck with him for the rest of his life.

Dear David,

It is so inspiring to see your heart for people. You are such a brave person! When no one else would fight for Israel you were willing and able. You stood up for your people. You offered yourself in the position of others. You were the savior of your people, standing in the gap for your nation. Your faithfulness saved lives. If you had not stood up for Israel many, many people would have died. It is true many owe their lives to you.

As you will learn, my dear David, leaders and great men are always criticized. Whenever one ventures to do a great thing there are always those who will stand aside to deride that leader. My dear David, please do not let this discourage you from your course. Do not let those action-less men dissuade you from your path. As men without courage often do, they must attempt to harm the reputation of the courageous to prop themselves up. I am convinced your path is the right one: Being courageous and trusting in the Lord is always the right path. Pay no attention to the men who stand aside, hands idle with mouths moving. Their actions are of no consequence and their words are equally fruitless.

God will shield you from any plot or weapon formed against you. My dear David, I am convinced that at the end of your days you will be declared victorious regardless of the many words the cowardly spoke against you. God will make you into a great man in His sight. Great men of God do not need to concern themselves with opinions of the untested. There are many with boasts but few with the mettle and skill to complete the necessary task.

As you feel inclined to discouragement, please remember this: You are a skilled young man. You are brave and God is with you. There is nothing the words of man can offer to increase your status with God, nor take away from it. Focus on fulfilling the call God has placed upon you and leave the talkers to talk.

The chief Philistine cities and their champions are both five. Keep your last four stones to complete the work you began with Goliath.

Sincerely,
Genesis Pilgrim

Traumatic Experience 3: <u>Forced Participation in Corpse Mutilation</u>

Read 1 Samuel 18:17-27

In this story David is serving as a commander within King Saul's army. After David's defeat of Goliath he was appointed as a military leader. Shortly after his rise within the army, Saul began to be jealous of David. So Saul began planning to kill David.

Rather than King Saul killing David directly, he set in motion events he guessed would have resulted in David's death. Saul told David he wanted to give his daughter to him in marriage. Then he gave his daughter in marriage to another man. Then Saul said he wanted to give David his next daughter in marriage. As a bridal gift Saul wanted David to kill a certain amount of Philistines to mutilate their bodies by removing their foreskins. We can only imagine the thoughts of David after being ordered to do such a disgusting thing.

However, as in other cases, David held back any objections and followed the orders of the king. He went to battle against the Philistines and mutilated their corpses as instructed.

We may choose to fault David here, but at this point we should remember David is perhaps still very young. When he fought the lion, the bear and Goliath, he was a boy. Shortly after this he finds himself appointed as a leader within the military. Then he is instructed to perform this gruesome task of corpse mutilation. When we understand David was likely a teenager we are able to see how he was taken advantage of by King Saul. David, being under orders and being very young, was unlikely to resist the order.

Ultimately Saul uses this task of corpse mutilation to humiliate David. This humiliation is extended further when the bridal gift is accepted by Saul, but later he takes away David's wife (see 1 Sam. 25:44). So within this short section we see David is the subject of waves of humiliation . . .

First, David is humiliated by being promised Saul's first daughter as his wife. Then Saul gives her to another man.

13

Second, the teenager David is humiliated by being ordered to perform a disgusting act of corpse mutilation.

Third, after David is married to Saul's second daughter, Saul takes her away from David and gives her to another man.

To make matters worse, these acts of humiliation were carried out through members in Saul's royal court. In 1 Sam. 18:22-26, Saul uses a type of peer pressure to convince David the act of corpse mutilation was acceptable. Within this context we can almost hear the attendants of Saul laughing and mocking David as they convince the naïve teenager to carry out the task of mutilation. It is no wonder David later suspects all people around him of plotting against him. David learned here at a young age that court officials would conspire against him.

In all these things, the humble, sincere, young David is the victim of a cruel king who manipulated him on the most intimate levels. David was offered two marriages and had both taken away. This would have furthered David's awkwardness with his relationships. Not only did David feel the weight of rejection from his parents, but now he was made to feel rejection twice in his prospects with marriage. And Saul did this by design—specifically trying to humiliate David because he was jealous of him.

In this way, the cruelty of Saul is greater than the cruelty of the lion and bear. Whereas the lion and bear each took a sheep to satisfy their appetite; Saul took away the wives of David for no purpose other than utterly shame him. In the midst of these humiliations, Saul also deliberately scarred David by demanding he perform an atrocity upon corpses. Thus, Saul deliberately afflicts David with unwanted upsetting memories of corpse mutilation.

The battlefield is sacred. All warriors should approach their task with the same gravity as a surgeon or a judge. The battlefield has never been a game to be treated idly. Any profession which concerns itself with the application of life and death needs to be humane. When a battle has been won, nothing can be gained by visiting further harm upon the dead or wounded. Saul scars the concept of the "righteous battlefield" within David—stripping away this concept of humane gravity. As a result of this mistreatment, David later struggles with some of his later decisions on various battlefields. Thus, Saul carries out a subconscious attack on David's future potential as a military commander by intentionally afflicting his mind.

Dear David,

When we are young we can be caught up in things we regret later. Your first step of healing is to admit to yourself what is wrong within these situations. Saul was wrong to ask you to mutilate the corpses. Regardless of whether or not corpse mutilation occurs at other times, you should have never been asked to do that. As you see these things as wrong, you can begin your journey of distancing yourself from the evil men who manipulated you in these situations. God offers us forgiveness for actions we have done and regret. All we need to do is repent, change our behavior and seek amends.

Sometimes we cannot change what we have done in the past. But we can admit what we did was wrong and refuse to do similar things again. We can also take actions to help others to avoid falling into the same bad behavior. If you would like to discuss different ways you can attempt to heal through this and make amends, I would like to discuss this with you.

Saul was also wrong for playing with your heart by offering his daughters then taking them away. In our previous discussion you stated you felt rejected by your parents from the moment of your birth—being cast solely upon the Lord. After the earlier rejections you suffered, it had to sting to have marriages waved before you only to have them ripped away. In this case you may feel as if there is something wrong with you. You may develop a very negative self-image—where you tell yourself you did something wrong to deserve all these broken relationships.

My dear David, you deserve love from your parents. You deserve a loving marriage. Sometimes things happen in our relationships that are beyond our control. It takes both people to make a relationship work. You were not rejected for anything you did wrong.

The rejections you experienced are a result of the shortcomings of other people. As a son you deserve to be loved. As a husband you deserve to be loved and to have your wife stay with you. Sometimes people give up on us for their own reasons. We cannot allow ourselves to bear responsibilities for the bad choices of others.

Do not despair. Do not give up on people. There are many good people who would love the opportunity to be your friend. When family does not want us, we are received by a family of faith which does. There are so many of us who have lost sons and daughters, who would love to have you as a member of our adopted family.

Do not despair of marriage. Although you may feel the sting of rejection now, this will pass. You deserve love.

Sincerely,
Genesis Pilgrim

Traumatic Experience 4: <u>Unnamed Battles</u>

Read 1 Samuel 18:5-7, 13, 30; 19:8 & Psalms 7, 35

In these Bible verses, David fights in many "unknown" battles. The location of the battles are not even recorded.

Although not much can be said, there is indeed something to be said of every battle fought by the warrior. Every time a warrior enters the arena he takes his life into his hands. Therefore we should approach all the memories of the warrior with the same sense of gravity—realizing there were many seemingly insignificant moments which could have resulted in the loss of everything for them.

David was such a strong warrior it became assumed he would be victorious in battle. David fought and won so many times his individual battles began to be viewed with a lack of significance. People simply praised and sang songs of the hero, yet there is no mention of personal concern for the person within the hero. Therefore, the legacy of the warrior often prevents him from receiving care for his common humanity. Thus, the warrior is abandoned to his purpose within the society he protects: he becomes a fighter—a person ever described as strong, never capable of weakness.

The negative aspect to being a skilled warrior is that eventually you are taken for granted. Your life begins to be viewed as no longer vulnerable. The terror you hold within as you enter the battle becomes yours alone. And due to this propping up received from others, the warrior is made to forget his own humanity.

Although others may sing of the warrior's battle prowess, the warrior must give heed to his humanity. The warrior needs to be reminded that it is okay for him to express human emotions, such as fear, grief, regret, sorrow and pain. When denying or pushing aside these emotions the warrior creates within himself a backlog of emotions.

Eventually the mind will force the warrior to cope with every emotion he "should" have felt, yet pushed aside. The battle-scarred warrior can become so proficient in his dealings with death that emotions no longer come naturally. As the warrior is trained to remove from himself every hindrance to the battlefield, he learns to push aside the basic human emotions which govern behavior. Thus the warrior gains battlefield prowess, but pays for it with portions of himself.

After a career of fighting for his society, the warrior often finds he no longer fits within it. After many battles where human emotions were pushed aside, those emotions can stop "speaking" to the mind of the warrior. The hits of battle jostle loose our minds' hold on the basic emotions that are a part of our humanity. Although a warrior may be inspiring and a citizen may be inclined to prop them up with praises, effort should be made to consider the "humanity" of the warrior. Do not prop up a warrior so he loses sight of his basic frame as a human.

So how does one reestablish emotions after undergoing trauma? When a warrior fights in so many battles that the battles themselves begin to blur—with nothing to distinguish one from another, how can the warrior find his way back? How can the warrior leave behind the "god-like" status imposed on him by fans as he learns to be "human" again? Here are some suggestions . . .

A warrior, or anyone who has went through tragedy, may need to take "baby steps" to re-capture the finesse of their emotions. The best way to begin this process is to match your emotions to your situation—allowing yourself to be moved by how you "feel." For example, if you are at a funeral, then grieve. Cry and let go of the things you have held onto.

Go back in time and re-play your memories with a counselor. If you did not have the time to experience the right emotions in past situations, then allow a counselor to coach you through those situations.

Let out your grief for those moments when you were not able to grieve. Allow yourself comfort. Tell yourself the truth: It was okay for you to be scared. It was okay for you to be terrified. It is okay for you to feel regret. Let those emotions come to the surface with your counselor. Allow yourself to step out of your invincible warrior armor. Allow yourself to feel as a human—to be vulnerable and not in complete control. By trusting a counselor, teach yourself that you do not have to stand in your own strength.

In supporting a warrior, or anyone who has went through tragedy, recognize that behind the impressive outer shell there is a person within. That person may have many struggles which have been pushed aside in the arena of war. Show love for the human person within.

Psalm 7 was likely written during this stage in David's life. Psalm 7 begins by mentioning a Benjamite, named Cush. Due to Saul being a Benjamite, it is likely this man was associated with Saul. It appears Cush levied false accusations against the young David (Psa. 7:1-5). David's military success began to make him the target of fellow officials within Saul's court. As each official vies for a higher position within the relatively new kingship of Israel under Saul, it is no surprise David would feel the pressure of these plots.

Here David prays to the Lord for help—asking him to vindicate him from the false charges. However, this is just the start of problems for David. Under increasing pressure, David later flees into the wilderness to escape the threats from Saul and his officials.

Similar to Psalm 7 above, Psalm 35 was likely written to commemorate the events leading up to David's decision to flee from King Saul. In Psalm 35:7-11, David states that certain people, which are likely officials in Saul's court, have levied false accusations against him. These officials also plotted against David in secret—mocking and slandering him (Psa. 35:15-21).

The mind of David was already scarred from many previous battles (1 Sam. 18:5-7). Thus, these waves of social persecution were devastating for the young shepherd David. His PTSD subconsciously developed protective mechanisms. These social persecutions led to the development of David's extreme social impairment. For the warrior David, cities became much more intimidating than battlefields. For the rest of David's life, he constantly suspected others of plotting against him.

Within these extreme social pressures, the young David grew immensely in his faith. In Psalm 35:1-6, David boldly asks the Angel of the

Lord to fight on his behalf—similar to how the Lord fought for Israel in the days of Moses and Joshua. Remarkably, the Spirit of the Lord directly intercedes to protect David. In Psalm 35:4, David asks the Lord to confuse and drive away those who pursue him. This prayer is answered when the Spirit of the Lord comes upon Saul and officials, compelling them to stop their pursuit to allow David to have more time to get away from them (1 Sam. 19:19-24).

Dear David,

Thank you for your willingness to serve your nation in many battles. Your work is appreciated and the nation owes itself to men like you. Your willingness to fight on behalf of your people allows citizens to live in peace and prosperity.

I realize how great a sacrifice is demanded of you every time you fight—even if there was nothing that history chose to record from those battles. If ever you would like to discuss any of your early battles, I would love the opportunity to learn from you. I am very interested in your struggles and successes and how God helped you to survive through each encounter with the enemy.

I realize too often warriors are expected to push aside all that hinders them from success. Often this means warriors do not have opportunity to properly grieve the loss of fellow soldiers. It also means warriors are so consumed with the task at hand that they are not able to fully process what happened, or to even enjoy brief moments of rest. If you would like to have a partner to grieve with, I will pray with you.

I understand warriors have to do much to "survive," so you will not receive any judgment from me. If you would like to get anything off your chest, please feel free to vent to me about anything you experienced or had to do to survive.

It is bittersweet to hear the praises people sing about us. Death and loss of life is never something praiseworthy. To celebrate the loss of thousands or tens of thousands is inhumane—to treat those who were lost in battle as mere numbers on a tally. By doing so it robs all on the battlefield of dignity. The deceased are robbed of their identity, reduced to only numbers and it is forgotten that they often fought out of government compulsion not evil intent. The victorious are robbed of dignity by songs praising their taking of life—which prevents them from maintaining the gravity of their task. All warriors must come eventually to account for the lives which they cut short. The songs of citizens hinder the warrior on that post-war, personal journey.

Indeed, how can one be brought to properly grieve for the result of his successful task when it is praised by the mass of citizens? Once again, we know death is never something to be celebrated. Humans should not be reduced to "numbers." And warriors, having completed the grave task of delivering punishment, should be allowed to move through stages of grief for friendly and foe alike. All deserve proper burial and the accompaniment of sincere prayer and grief—even if the laws of the Earth happened to designate one as an "enemy." Although we deal death to enemies, we should not allow inhumane thoughts concerning them to arise in our hearts—encouraged by the masses of our citizens. Grieve for all human losses—friend and foe.

War is so complicated, my dear David. Please do not feel as if you are alone in carrying the burden of your experiences. If you would like to speak with me, I welcome discussing any of your experiences with you. You will receive no judgment from me.

Sincerely,
Genesis Pilgrim

Traumatic Experience 5: Eluding Capture from King Saul

Read 1 Samuel 19:9-21:1 & Psalms 17, 55, 59, 139

In this Bible passage, Saul attempts to kill David with a spear. After being unsuccessful in 1 Sam. 18:10-11 and 19:10-11, Saul orders his attendants to have David arrested. David's wife warns him of the plot and he escapes the city.

Although David appears alone, at each location he has an ally. Before David fled from the city, Jonathan defended David to the king (1 Sam. 19:1-7). In the city, his wife was his ally. When David travelled to the cities of Ramah and Naioth, Samuel the prophet was with him (1 Sam. 19:18). Then when David moves to the field, Jonathan meets him (1 Sam. 20:1-42). Last, in the city of Nob, the priest Ahimelech helped David (1 Sam. 20:1-9). This is important because although David is oppressed and fleeing for his life, God provides him an ally in each location.

In addition to these allies, the Spirit of the Lord also moves upon Saul and his men to disrupt their pursuit of David (1 Sam. 19:19-23). In this way, God answers the prayer of David in Psalm 59 by Himself arising to deliver David (Psa. 59:4). God uses the lips of David's pursuers against them—compelling them to prophesy (Psa. 59:7-8). This allows David more time to create distance from his pursuers.

Psalm 59 was written by David to describe this event in his life. Within city walls there should be protection for citizens. However in Psalm 59, David describes the servants of Saul who were seeking him. In this way the safety of the city becomes a battlefield for David. This leads him to later suspect those who are whispering of plotting against him.

Psalm 55 describes a similar situation, but in Psalm 55 David even suspects his closest friend of betraying him. Perhaps this shows us that during his fleeing David had moments where he even suspected Jonathan of betrayal. Of course this was untrue, but it serves to show us how deeply this assault from Saul affected David's mind. As he fled, he imagined all had betrayed him. To counter this downward spiral within David's mind, God is faithful to provide an ally for David in each location he travels. God wants David to see that despite conditions appearing hopeless, there is always a remnant of the faithful who will reach out to preserve lovingkindness. Thus we can be encouraged. Although we may feel alone and betrayed, God will send people to rally us.

In this life there is much beyond comprehension. The cruelty of King Saul is something so puzzling it left David with prayer as his only option. At times we have problems that are so big and confusing all we can do is ask God to do "something" about it—being so unsure within ourselves of anything we could do to improve our situation. The young David was indeed stuck in an impossible situation—where the king cruelly despised and oppressed David for no crime, but for simply being himself.

Psalm 17 captures this sentiment. Here David looks to God as his refuge in the midst of being surrounded by those who desire to hurt him. At the end of Psalm 17, David asks God to awaken him from this bad dream. When we understand the battle-scarred mind of David, it makes sense he would view these impossibly difficult situations of rejection as a "dream." This would allow him to somehow distance himself from his reality so he could survive.

We must remember it is the king himself who is oppressing David. So David has no means of recourse or justice. He is indeed stuck—day after day, moment after moment. He must find a way to cope in the midst of danger he could not escape.

The symptoms of a PTSD panic attack can be severe. David imagined the plots of others so clearly it caused physical symptoms. In Psalm 55, David imagines others plotting to betray him. Accompanying these thoughts are serious physical symptoms. In Psalm 55:2-17, David says he has: (1) a heart in anguish, (2) overwhelming fear, trembling and horror, and (3) emotional distress which continues for days—evening, morning and noon. These are all symptoms typical among those who are experiencing PTSD trauma. It is not that the plotting of the people is causing the distress within David, but that his mind creates a situation in which the thoughts are so real they emerge in physical symptoms. David explains in Psalm 55 he would have symptoms that would persist for days.

To protect itself, the mind of David begins to view his surroundings as a "dream." This is necessary because the mind cannot allow the heart to race unchecked. Eventually the mind of the person with PTSD must take action to re-frame reality to allow the person to survive.

Therefore within David's mind emerges the new reality of God as the true reality. David here develops the ability to toggle in and out of physical reality. When David's mind begins to overreact to its physical environment, the mind automatically begins to override—allowing David to experience the spiritual reality where God is his fortress and stronghold.

This is how David learns to "walk by faith, not by sight." This is why David often speaks of God as his refuge, stronghold and fortress throughout the Psalms. At the beginning of Psalm 59 it states it is written in memory of David's experience of eluding capture. Then in Psalm 59:9-16, God is referred to as a refuge and stronghold.

The traumatic experiences of David grant him a new ability—which is absolutely critical for those with faith. David gains the ability to move between the physical and spiritual world in his mind—and when things become too impossible for his mind to grasp he becomes able to visualize inwardly the "fortress" of God which surrounds and protects him. He becomes capable of escaping to this spiritual reality (Psalm 55:7-8).

At the core of what it means to be a Christian is the ability to focus one's mind on the unseen spiritual kingdom of God. Ultimately this ability can be traced to combat trauma. When one's mind is overwhelmed by the physical reality surrounding it, the mind develops the ability to think of the spiritual world. Perhaps this is why the Lord Jesus tells us to reach out to those on the fringes of society—the imprisoned, sick, hungry and needy (Matt. 25:31-46). For within this group are found people who have likely come to the realization that this physical world is one which needs to be escaped somehow. And through faith in the unseen—walking by faith, not by sight—one can set aside the physical in preference for the spiritual reality of God.

Although David continues to struggle with his thoughts, his ability to see the unseen fortress of God is the means through which David is able to survive it all.

Would you like to see what it is like for David to be within God's refuge? Psalm 139 gives us a detailed description of how David would feel as the physical reality of his surroundings was swallowed up by his mind's presentation of the spiritual reality. The fortress of God is one within the mind of all believers. It is a place where we can honestly vent our aggression and anxious thoughts (Psa. 139:21-23). In this place a believer can speak to the Lord candidly, receiving help in whatever hardship they face.

Dear David,

I am saddened to hear of your situation. I understand how you feel so trapped and helpless—being unable to escape. It is one thing to endure a temporary evil for a moment, but when that evil becomes an inescapable reality it is too much for our minds to bear.

I am very happy to hear you have found comfort in the Lord during this time. Your example helps me to see no matter how difficult the physical circumstances around us may appear we have a refuge . . . a fortress . . . and a stronghold which is unseen and mightier than all things.

Your example shows how you were able to survive all battles and all traps set for you by evil men. It is amazing to think how the kingdom of God is found within us as we shift our focus off the physical world to the spiritual. We can find ourselves in the hottest battle and this kingdom of God found within us can provide us incredible strength and courage to endure it with success. Truly this is why all battles belong to the Lord. Battles are not won through physical strength. Rather, battles are won as the mind turns momentarily from the physical, to be energized in the spiritual, then to apply that spiritual strength to the physical. Thank you for showing me this, David.

I also learned if a mind is affected by PTSD it opens them up to the possibility of the spiritual reality. We must become dissatisfied with this physical world in order to be saved from it. You mentioned the anguish of your heart and your enduring panic at the thought of being betrayed. Although it can be debilitating to have our hearts change rhythm, this symptom teaches us the hard truth: physical life is fleeting. We must learn to trust God as early as possible. I am so encouraged to see you have learned this.

Also my dear friend, do not give up on people. Even when it seems that all have betrayed us, God will always preserve a remnant of faithful to stand by our sides. I am encouraged to hear Jonathan, Samuel and Ahimelech provided help to you during your latest trial. May you be blessed friend until we speak again.

Sincerely,
Genesis Pilgrim

Traumatic Experience 6: <u>Captured by Philistines</u>

Read 1 Samuel 21:10-15 & Psalms 31, 34, 56

In this story David is captured and brought before the Philistine king, Achish. At this time David was alone, and it was likely he was arrested by Philistines. Thinking they would receive an award for the capture of David, the citizens of Gath bring them to the Philistine king.

This is an especially dangerous situation for David. When the judge, Samson, was captured by the Philistines, they blinded him (Judg. 16:20-21). It is likely David knew what happened to Samson because elsewhere in the Bible it explains he had knowledge of other historical events (2 Sam. 11:20-21). In this passage David finds himself in a similar situation. Therefore he must do everything he can to escape this danger.

Psalm 56 was written to commemorate David's experience in this Bible passage. At the end of the psalm, David says the Lord delivered him from death in this situation. Thus, David was convinced he would have been put to death by King Achish.

Psalm 34 was also written to commemorate David's experience here. In Psalm 34:7-8, David says the Lord is a refuge of protection. In David's mind, although he was surrounded by enemies, the Angel of the Lord was surrounding the entire city of Gath. This means he had nothing to fear as he reflects back upon this experience.

Psalm 31 states it was written when David was in a city surrounded by enemies. It is likely David is referring to his experience of being arrested and brought before the Philistine king. In Psalm 31:4-8, David says he committed his spirit to the Lord in the midst of the many idol-worshippers. As a result the Lord rescues him from the hand of his enemies and puts him in a spacious place. In this way, God ensures the escape of David.

So what did David do to ensure he could escape?

David uses deception to escape this situation. When brought before the king, David pretends to be a mad man—making marks on the walls and letting saliva run down his beard. This is sufficient to convince Achish that

31

either David is not the man he expected or the mad man before him was not the real David. Either way, David escapes the fate of Samson.

Dear David,

It must have been terrifying to be arrested by the Philistines. I am so happy you made it out of that place.

I notice these bad events are occurring in waves. You had one sheep attacked by a lion, then you had one attacked by a bear. You were insulted by your brother Eliab in the army camp, then you were insulted by Saul, then insulted by Goliath. You had one wife taken away, then another wife.

At times it seems bad times stack upon one another. Often this brings us to the point where we are overwhelmed. But these bad events can teach us to place our hope in God. In bad times continue looking to God for deliverance.

Many men live in contentment, being unconcerned with the spiritual world around them. When they are not sent trouble and bad times they find no occasion for faith. Thus they remain evermore physical creatures. So we see when the Lord allows hard times these are used to discipline us. And every child who has a good parent endures discipline. When you endure these terrible times which try your mind, be encouraged! These hardships demonstrate you are a dear son of God. Over time it will become clearer these experiences demonstrate God's faithfulness, love and concern for you.

In our past discussions you said you feel rejected by your parents from the moment of your birth—being cast upon the Lord from the womb. Indeed your experiences are showing that God Himself is your Father. Although you experience persecution, your Father is faithful to deliver you from them all. The fortress of God will stand fast. All waves will break upon it. Take refuge in the supernatural stronghold of the Lord, my dear David.

I am confident of good things for you, David. God has answered your prayer by adopting you into His family. I am excited for your future. May your faith overwhelm every trouble you face. Every battle belongs to the Lord. Continue to trust him, my friend.

Sincerely,
Genesis Pilgrim

Traumatic Experience 7: <u>Compelled to Leave Parents in Moab Stronghold</u>

Read 1 Samuel 22:1-5 & Psalm 86

In this passage, people rally around David while he is at the Cave of Adullam. David becomes a commander over a group of 400 fighting men—who were previously distressed, discontent or in debt.

David's parents and brothers hear he is at the cave, so they come to him as well. After being reunited with his family, David travelled to Mizpah in Moab to ask the king to allow his parents to stay in the city.

At this point, David's parents were elderly. In 1 Samuel 17:12-18 it explains that Jesse, David's father, was old and advanced in years. It might be they needed a caretaker.

The old age of David's parents may have contributed to his lack of connection with them. In the Psalms we discussed David's feelings of rejection and how he felt as if he was cast upon the Lord from the moment of his birth (Psa. 22:9-10; 27:10; 69:8). This might have been due to David's parents being too old to care for David, and overly relying on him as the family shepherd and errand runner.

It is comforting to see in this passage David had opportunity for this family reunion. Following this passage there is no further mention of his parents, so we are left to assume they may have passed away shortly after this.

At the end of this passage, the prophet Gad tells David not to remain in the stronghold of Moab. David asks the king of Moab to look after his parents as he sets out with his army of 400 men.

Earlier we discussed how David developed the PTSD ability to visualize the spiritual fortress of God. Since David has learned to trust in the kingdom of God for his protection, the prophet Gad fittingly encourages him to leave behind the need for man-made fortresses. The presence of Gad encourages David to trust in the Lord for protection.

Psalm 86 may commemorate this Bible passage. In Psalm 86:16, David is sentimental—declaring the inspiration he has gained from his mother's faith. This is different than other passages where David typically discusses his parents in a negative light—focusing on their rejection of him (1 Sam. 16:11 & Psa. 22:10; 27:10; 69:8). Perhaps this change occurred during David's visit with his parents in the Moab stronghold. Psalm 86:16 seems to indicate this visit was a positive influence for David where some healing occurred from past family problems.

There are other clues in Psalm 86 which may indicate this psalm was written to commemorate 1 Samuel 22:1-5. David describes himself as a needy man—which fits his situation where he was sojourning as a foreigner (Psa. 86:1). Due to King Saul pursuing him, David cries out to God for protection in his constant state of distress (Psa. 86:2-7, 14). Within the Moab stronghold, David reflects on the Lord's greatness compared to the "gods" of other nations (Psa. 86:8-9). David trusts God to guard his life—confident the Lord will continue to deliver him from death as He has done in the past (Psa. 86:2, 13).

Dear David,

In our previous discussions we talked about your parents and your perception of them. It is encouraging to hear you had this opportunity to meet again with your parents and your brothers. After going through some difficult times, where you were right to feel rejected and insulted, it took tremendous courage for you to offer yourself to your family again in this meeting.

Although we have not discussed how your family reunion went, I hope this was a time of restoration and healing. Maybe your brothers apologized to you for wrongs. Maybe your parents told you how much they love you. Let me tell you again . . . You are a great son and any parent would be blessed to have you as a son. You are a hard-worker, brave, a strong warrior, a great leader and a man of God. Your parents should be proud of you!

Your treatment of your fellow men shows your quality. Do you remember when I told you that your love for your sheep—and your desire to protect them, even if it meant fighting a lion and a bear with your hands, would be the quality that makes you a great leader? Here we see your care for those on the fringes of society. Rather than giving up on the men who are in debt, distressed and discouraged, you chose to offer them purpose. You gave them a reason to fight for another chance at life. You provided hope for these 400 men in the same way you gave hope to the sheep as they were carried off.

I am encouraged to see you have Gad the prophet with you. Any good leader needs good counselors. You are not forsaken. There are many people God will put in your path to help you in every deed to which you are called. Over time use all opportunities to surround yourself with good, proficient, faithful people. They will provide counsel to you in difficult times. God will use them for good in many ways. Whenever you find a man or woman of quality, work to persuade them to join with you in your calling. I trust this will help you in times of need.

Please continue to look for opportunities to extend mercy. You have such a large heart. Allow that compassion to guide all your actions, my dear David.

Sincerely,
Genesis Pilgrim

Traumatic Experience 8: Saul Executes Nob Citizens

Read 1 Samuel 22:6-23 & Psalm 52

While still pursuing David in order to kill him, King Saul discovers David received help from the priests at the city of Nob. After speaking with the priest, Saul issues the order to execute the priests and people of Nob. When Saul's men were unwilling to kill the priests, a foreigner named Doeg did it.

One of the priests, named Abiathar, escaped and fled to David. Upon his arrival, Abiathar reported to David that the priests and people of Nob were killed. Then David takes responsibility for the sequence of events he set in motion when he asked for help from the priests. David blames himself for putting the priests and people of Nob at risk by passing through that city. As a result, David offers Abiathar a permanent place within his company. From this point on, Abiathar becomes a counselor for David.

David does not take the time necessary to grieve the loss of the priests. Due to him needing to flee from Saul to survive, David is not able to get any closure following the deaths of the priests. This affects his mind as he is left with the guilt of thinking himself responsible for the tragedy, yet lacking the ability to properly come to terms with the reality of the situation. Thus over the coming years his mind maintains the false belief he was responsible for the destruction of Nob.

In later times of loss, David takes the time to properly grieve. Funerals are not for the dead. Funerals are for the living. They give us the opportunity to consider what happened, to celebrate the life of the person lost and to consider how our lives were touched by them. Due to David missing out on this opportunity to grieve properly, the false belief of his guilt was left to fester within his mind for years. This is why it is so important to come to terms with losses. By doing so it gives us the chance to correctly frame events within our minds.

During funerals, stories are told by others. These stories serve to inform us on where we fit within the story of the person who was lost.

Whereas David thought himself responsible for the deaths of the priests, attendance of a funeral would have challenged this false belief. If David were able to visit Nob, he would have seen the destruction. He would have heard from multiple people that Saul and Doeg were responsible for the deaths which occurred there. Over the course of hearing multiple stories, David would have been moved gently to a proper understanding of the events which took place at Nob.

Although David passed through Nob, he never "intended" for this to hurt anyone. Also David did not order the deaths of the priests, or carry out the executions. Other people were responsible for those things. In this way the denial of opportunity to grieve creates problems within the mind of David. Rather than properly framing the tragic events, he is left to think himself culpable. Worse, every time he sees Abiathar it serves as a reminder of this false reality. Whenever he sees Abiathar his mind brings him back to the false reality: He is to blame for the deaths of Abiathar's family.

Psalm 52 was later written by David to commemorate the events of this Bible passage. Later it is seen within this psalm David comes to terms with his grief. The first sections of Psalm 52 are addressed to Doeg—the evil man who was truly responsible for the deaths. Psalm 52 concludes by David seeing himself as a neutral party. David describes himself as an olive tree in the house of God. David initially sees himself as responsible for the deaths of the priests, but later (perhaps many years later) he is brought to the realization he was innocent of the crime committed at Nob.

Perhaps it is through later funerals David learns this and properly reframes the events of Nob within his mind. Later when grieving for the deaths of others (Saul, Jonathan, Abner and Absalom), David no longer places blame upon himself for deaths of others where he was not involved. Instead David places responsibility directly upon those who actually raised the weapons to cause the deaths. When comparing the events of Nob to these later losses, the main difference is that David had opportunity to properly grieve; whereas concerning the Nob incident he was prevented from attending a funeral.

Thus we see the trauma that can occur within the mind when a person is denied opportunity to grieve through a funeral. War does not allow breaks as the individual is repeatedly faced with situations in which they must continue to fight and survive. Therefore soldiers often are not able to come to terms with losses. As a result, the mind of the soldier can build within it a "false reality" where the person holds themselves responsible for events they truly did not "intend" and for which they cannot rightly bear responsibility. We learn this from the experience of David.

Dear David,

I am saddened to hear about the loss of people at Nob.

My dear friend, you are not responsible for this. These people were killed by Saul and Doeg. You did not, and never would, raise a weapon against any of the priests and their families.

When you arrived at Nob, you never "intended" to cause any harm to the citizens there. This is important for you to remember now. At no time did you imagine evil upon the priests. So within your heart you are absolutely innocent—and you need to admit this.

The loss of life is tragic, and we can mourn, grieve and cry for it. But as a part of this grief I will not allow you to take blame upon yourself. The blame is to be placed exclusively on man who issued the order (Saul), and the man who raised the weapon (Doeg). You are as innocent as an olive tree in the house of God.

We should join with Abiathar, the priest, in grieving for the loss of his family. Although you are not permitted time to stop your travels to grieve, take time to do this. Spend time mourning with Abiathar. As you move beyond the days of mourning, listen to Abiathar as he tells you stories about his family. Ask him questions and help him in treasuring those memories. God sent him to you for a mutual blessing. You can help one another to properly grieve this loss.

Do you remember how we discussed your relationship with your own parents? You explained how you felt rejected and cast upon the Lord from the moment of your birth. Although you are different from Abiathar, your stories are intersecting with one another. You experienced in part a loss of your family and now Abiathar is also experiencing a loss of his own family. It is a terrible situation, but God is bringing you together to help one another. You need a family who will receive you, and Abiathar is also in need of a family.

Just as you rescued the sheep back from the paws of the lion and the bear, now rescue Abiathar from the hands of the wicked. Welcome him into your flock. Extend to him mercy and kindness. Just as you served faithfully to bring the injured sheep back to health, so also you can serve to faithfully bring the injured Abiathar back to health.

There is no need to assign yourself blame for this tragedy, my dear David. You were not responsible for the cruelty of the lion and bear that caused the harming of the sheep. Likewise you are not responsible for the cruelty of evil men who killed the priests at Nob.

Your compassion is so inspiring. You are a brave, strong warrior. Do not become consumed with the motives that led to the damaging of the sheep. At this point let go of that. Mourn and grieve. Cry.

Sincerely,
Genesis Pilgrim

Traumatic Experience 9: <u>Philistine Battle at Keilah & Fear of Capture by Saul</u>

Read 1 Samuel 23:1-13

Shortly after the priest Abiathar arrived in David's camp, the Philistines attacked a nearby city, called Keilah. David goes to Abiathar to pray with him for guidance on what they should do. The Lord God directs David to go to Keilah to save it from the Philistine army. When his soldiers attempted to dissuade David from God's direction, David chose to be obedient to God instead.

David and his army defeated the Philistines. Once inside the walled city of Keilah, David receives a report that King Saul may attempt to capture him at Keilah. Being unsure of the best choice in this situation, David once again prays with the priest Abiathar. The Lord makes it clear Saul will capture David if he remains in the city. God explains the citizens of Keilah will arrest David and deliver him to Saul. So, David and his group of 600 warriors choose to leave Keilah to camp in the wilderness.

Whereas David acted out of pure motive to help the citizens of Keilah, God informs him that those same people will arrest him and deliver him to King Saul. In this way this story is a reversal of the earlier arrest and capture of David when he was brought before Achish in Gath. Both accounts describe David as being within a city of people who will betray him to death before a king.

Instantly the mind of David makes the connection between his present circumstances and his earlier close call with death when captured in Gath. After rescuing Keilah, David's anxiety builds as he finds himself within a city where he could be trapped if besieged by Saul.

The vision God grants David is very precise. Psalm 31 may refer to this experience in part, with the details of David's earlier arrest in Gath being blurred with his anxiety in Keilah. In Psalm 31:21-22, David declares he was in a city under siege. In other words, God granted David a vision of what would happen if he chose to remain in Keilah. David immediately responded to the vision and removed himself from danger.

When considering the mind of the warrior with PTSD, the experience of David makes sense. Prior to this experience, David had two "close calls" with death within cities. The first was when David was nearly captured by Saul when soldiers were sent to arrest him in his bedroom. The second was when David nearly suffered the fate of Samson when he was arrested and brought before Achish, the Philistine king of Gath.

The PTSD mind automatically connects the dots with similar situations in order to protect itself. Being within the walled city of Keilah immediately gave David waves of anxiety. He automatically suspected the citizens of Keilah would betray him. In this way, the anxiety of David prompts him to pray for guidance. Following his initial thoughts, God confirms to him it is dangerous for him to remain in the city. David wastes no time in being obedient to the vision from God. He and his army of 600 move out of the city and back into the wilderness.

Some may view the effects of PTSD as a disability. But for the warrior, the changes which occur within the mind and body as a result of PTSD are life-saving. PTSD provides the warrior with intuitive prompts to ensure survival. When David could not "consciously" sense danger, his mind "subconsciously" interpreted the situation as dangerous (Psa. 31:9-10, 22). Those with PTSD can have severe physical symptoms which drive them to remove themselves from dangerous situations. Within the Psalms, David mentions changes in his heart often—which is likely a reference to the fast heart beat that accompanies panic attacks. David also mentions symptoms of anxiety as he suspects the plots of others and mentally predicts the actions of those around him.

These are all the symptoms of a proficient, battle-hardened warrior. The heart of the warrior races to give his muscles a surge of strength as the body poises itself for a fight. A racing heart is a good survival mechanism because it gives the warrior a jump start before his opponent has opportunity to begin the fight. Anxiety also gives the warrior a jump start because it helps him to predict the next move of his opponent and allows him to plot his counter move.

In this, the behavior of David is exactly what we would expect of a warrior. His warrior mind feeds him helpful doses of anxiety and physical responses to prepare him to survive what will come next.

As David progresses in his spiritual journey, he learns to use these common PTSD symptoms to grow closer to God. When his heart beats faster and when his anxiety rises, he uses these as cues to start praying. In this Bible story we get a glimpse of how David uses PTSD symptoms to grow more responsive and closer to God. When he feels intense anxiety this prompts him to go to God for guidance.

David's PTSD symptoms provide subconscious shifts in his perception from the natural to a stunning enhancement of the natural world with supernatural power. As time progresses, David develops further the ability to vitalize himself through his supernatural perception of God's protection. When in a perceived dangerous situation, David's mind shifts—allowing him to instantly draw supernatural power from God, importing it with him back into his physical surroundings. Thus, PTSD in the ancient warrior is a powerful enabling ability that gives the individual a burst of strength.

Dear David,

You are so compassionate and brave! When hearing about the Philistine attack on the city of Keilah, you looked to God for strength then ran in to rescue the people. This is exactly what I would expect from the same brave boy who threw off all fear—being compelled by love to rescue his sheep from the lion and bear.

As a boy you rescued sheep. As a man you rescue men who are destitute—placing them in your army. Now, you are rescuing cities!

I am encouraged to hear Abiathar is your trusted ally. Shortly after his arrival in your camp, I can see you are praying with the priest often. You prayed with him for guidance concerning the decisions to rescue Keilah and also when to leave the city. I hope in the future you will continue to look to the faithful priest and prophets within your company. They will help you keep your eyes on the Lord.

I saw when God directed you to fight Keilah, some of the men attempted to dissuade you from following God's direction. At times God may direct us to do things that do not make sense to others. Pay no attention to people when their words move to discourage you from the path God has placed before you. Fight the battles the Lord gives you and do not give way to fear. As leaders we can receive input from various counselors, but ultimately the leader has to make the right decision. When God gives us clear guidance this should be followed above all else. Remember the Judges. Look to Moses and Joshua. Unwavering faith maintains courage.

As warriors, within us a fire rages: Although all is silent, our hearts gallop and our minds race forward. With youth this is a difficult thing to master. It is a difficult thing to understand. But turn this intensity into a supernatural source of power. When the fires rage and the heart gallops, use this as a prompt to see the fortress of the Lord around you.

The intense surges are echoes of the angelic kingdom which stirs as the weapons of God are raised to do battle on our behalf. The kingdom of heaven is within you—with your mind moving you to embrace this spiritual reality. I will pray you continue to see this more and more clearly, my dear David.

Betrayal is never easy to endure. It is great to hear God removed you from Keilah before the citizens had an opportunity to repay your kindness with evil. In all places remain no longer than necessary to accomplish the task God sets before you in that place. After God calls you to a place, be mindful when he calls you to depart.

In this way your journeys in the wilderness may reflect those of Israel during the Exodus. Remain in each place while the cloud rests. But keep your eyes on the spiritual cloud—that heavenly fortress, stronghold and refuge, my dear David. When it rises, move with it. Remain ever under its protection and give no room for yourself to be abused outside of its canopy. May God grant you wisdom to ever see the fortress and to follow it faithfully, my friend.

> *Sincerely,*
> *Genesis Pilgrim*

Traumatic Experience 10: <u>Escape from Saul at the Desert of Maon</u>

Read 1 Samuel 23:19-28 & Psalms 54, 63

In this Bible passage, David was camping in the Desert of Ziph. Saul's son, Jonathan, secretly visited David and encouraged him. Then the people of Ziph went secretly to King Saul to betray David. Upon receiving this report, Saul sets out to capture David with his army.

The passage ends with Saul being in close pursuit of David. In a mountain region, David could see Saul's army from a distance, moving ever closer. However, as Saul's army neared David's company, Saul received a report of war within the territory of Israel. So Saul immediately stopped pursuing David and turned back. In this way David escaped capture.

Two psalms were later written by David to commemorate his experiences in this passage. Psalm 63 addresses David's time within the desert. This was a time of spiritual growth for David. The psalm mentions David's praises and reflections upon God's protection and provision. For in this time he could briefly rejoice he was free of enemies. Within the desert, God teaches David to trust in the natural fortresses of the rocks and more importantly in the spiritual Rock of the Lord (1 Sam.23:14, 28).

Throughout Scripture, the wilderness is a place of spiritual growth. The desert is often a place where a man of God can go, become spiritually refreshed and prepared for the next journey. In this passage and Psalm 63 we find this is the case for David as well. When deprived of water and food, one is compelled to look for nourishment from another source. Therefore, the desert is a natural place where spiritual growth can occur.

However, the betrayal of the people of Ziph shatter David's spiritual respite. Psalm 54 commemorates the thoughts of David following his receipt of the report that he had been betrayed by the people of Ziph. We see a sharp contrast between Psalm 63 and Psalm 54. In Psalm 63, David is peaceful. But in Psalm 54, after the betrayal of Ziph his anxiety awakens.

In Psalm 63, David shifts his focus to those who betrayed him. He asks God to deliver him and to punish his enemies. So, David is brought from the solace of inner, self-reflection in Psalm 63 back into an anxiety-filled survival mode in Psalm 54. The betrayal removes David from his "mountain top" experience of spiritual growth and drags him back down into the "valley" of anxiety and despair. David must prepare to flee once again.

Dear David,

It is often said in this life we have both mountain top experiences and experiences where we are in the lowest valley. It is encouraging to hear you had a brief respite from your anxiety. You were able to rest for a time in the desert—focusing on God. But as is the case with all such mountain top experiences, they are often given to us to prepare us for the next struggle we will face.

In the same fashion which afflicts all people of faith—while you were captured in praise and spiritual reflection, a trial emerged. It is never easy to endure the evil of men, and betrayal is one of the worst evils.

In the past I know you have struggled with your doubt of people—suspecting them of plotting against you. It is terrible the people of Ziph wronged you in this way because it may serve to make you more withdrawn from people. However, please do your best to avoid thinking too much about the betrayal you suffered here. There are many people of faith whom you can trust. Do not give up altogether on account of the betrayal of the faithless.

One of the things I have learned from our discussions is that the fortress, stronghold and refuge of the Lord is not at a specific location. This kingdom is within all those who have faith in the Lord. This is important to remember. As you are made to move from one location to another, do not think God is sending you away from His Presence. Rather, think of the Presence of God being within you and above you—sustaining you inwardly, and moving as a vast fortress of protection with you.

This fortress of the Lord moves ahead of you, stays with you and also guards your rear to protect you from all sides. You may feel as if you are being chased away from the good place of rest and worship. However this is allowed to occur to show you that you do not depend on a specific location. As you travel, the same attitude of high worship and praise travels within you. It is the same fortress which protected you as Saul closed in to capture you.

Please remember this, my dear David. The desert of spiritual growth cannot be found on a map. It is a "desert" within the heart of the faithful. It is a place of retreat which provides you with strength from within. In all your future travels, my friend, look in faith to this desert fortress of the Lord—where you are nourished and protected from all harm.

Sincerely,

Genesis Pilgrim

Traumatic Experience 11: <u>Escape from Saul in Cave</u>

Read 1 Samuel 24:1-15 & Psalms 57, 142

In this Bible passage, King Saul begins to look for David in the Desert of En Gedi. David and some of his men were hiding in a cave. Then, as Saul happened upon that place, he went into the same cave looking for a place to relieve himself.

David refused to harm Saul because he was "anointed" by the Lord. This "anointing" is significant. First, it is significant because in Israel's history, the Judges were the anointed by the Lord. This occurred when "the Spirit of the Lord came upon" each judge. In the book of Judges, God would raise up and empower a judge in successive generations. Each judge was appointed to a specific task in order to rescue Israel in some way. Although the judges all had personal flaws, they each played a necessary part within Israel's history.

So, David's refusal to harm the Lord's "anointed" is connected to this historical knowledge of the Judges. Although Saul had personal flaws, David was convinced if he were to kill Saul before his full purpose appointed by God was accomplished then David might be dooming the entire nation to destruction.

Moreover, David was "anointed" with the same anointing as Saul— being both anointed by Samuel. Thus, if David were to take action to kill Saul, then it would set a precedent for someone to do the same to him. Therefore, the rule to avoid laying a hand on the Lord's anointed was intended to provide preservation to God's work among the nation through each future anointed ruler.

While Saul was in the cave, some of David's men urged him to kill Saul. David instead cuts off a piece of Saul's clothing. After Saul moves away from the cave, David calls out to him. David shows the piece of cloth he cut from his garment—demonstrating he had the opportunity to kill Saul yet did not.

David then states God will serve as the Judge—knowing that David is blameless in his behavior toward Saul even when he is threatened with death. David vows his hand will not be raised against Saul.

The mention of God as Judge is significant. In his response, David refers to the Lord as the Judge twice. Keeping in mind the position of "king" was new in Israel, David likely viewed Saul and himself as being within the succession of Judges. So if one judge had a dispute with another judge, then they would appeal to the Supreme Judge for a decision—similar to how subordinate judges would bring the harder cases before Moses for judgment (Exo. 18:22). In this way, David appeals to the Lord Himself to vindicate him—declaring him innocent of wrongdoing.

Within the context it is amazing Saul was so intent on killing David. In the previous chapter, Saul is chasing David before he is called away to fight the Philistines. Then as soon as Saul completes this battle with the Philistines, he returns immediately to his pursuit of David. When considering Saul's leadership of the entire nation, it is incredible he devoted so much attention to his pursuit of David in the wilderness. Why indeed should the king of an entire nation be personally involved with the pursuit of a single man in the desert?

To bring attention to this point, David refers to himself as a "dead dog" and a "flea" as a part of his appeal for Saul to leave him alone. In this, David greatly underestimates himself as a "dog" or a "flea." He was so important the king himself remained in the wilderness—just to find David.

It could be David was just being humble, but it is more likely David had low self-esteem. We see this low self-esteem in David's early life. He is rejected by his parents and left in the field during the visit of Samuel the prophet. David is ridiculed by his brother in the army camp. He is told he is an unexperienced boy by King Saul when he boldly volunteers to fight Goliath. Then Goliath ridicules David on the battlefield—referring to him as a stick that is waved before a dog.

At the core of David's upbringing is the persisting thought that he is insignificant. Therefore, when David underestimates himself in the Psalms and elsewhere, he is not merely being humble. Rather he is interacting with a deep seated belief rooted in his childhood trauma. He thought of himself as rejected and despised. Although he was a successful warrior, his life was full of social rejection and social anxiety—where he often suspected others of plotting against him.

In these things we see a social awkwardness common among warriors with PTSD. David is physically powerful on the battlefield, yet he crumbles in social settings. This is shown clearly in his writing within the Psalms. He presents others who are plotting against him as superior to himself (Psa. 142:6). He believes himself helpless to protect himself, routinely asking the Lord to help him. This makes it clear that although David was a powerful warrior, he viewed himself as the weaker when placed in the company of citizens who were not under his military authority.

This view of others is a defense mechanism of PTSD. When a warrior is subject to repeated insults and rejection, his PTSD mind begins to prepare itself for the next social threat. In other words, social settings become a battlefield. The battle-scarred mind of David copes with potential danger by giving him subconscious social insecurities, leading him to imagine all whispers are from people plotting his destruction. By doing so, the PTSD mind of David attempts to protect him by giving an edge on anyone who would come against him. The mind anticipates the cruel actions of all around it so it can be poised to defend itself when any potential enemy begins to make his first move.

In the Bible there are two psalms where David commemorates his experiences within the cave. In Psalm 57:4, David explains those who seek him have many weapons and traps set to kill him. Yet, God demonstrates his power by leading the enemy himself to become trapped by his own devices. Saul desired to trap and capture David, yet God allowed Saul himself to become trapped and captured before David in the cave.

Throughout David's writings in the Psalms, David consistently asks God to return the evil deeds of people back upon themselves. In David's mind, God's justice turns back upon the evil doer. God metes out upon them "exactly" the same misfortunes they designed for the innocent. In this psalm we see an exact picture of God's justice. Saul sought to trap David and take his life, so God trapped Saul and delivered his life to David. In this, God is absolutely "just"—doing nothing more, and nothing less than what the evil doer deserves.

Psalm 142 was also written to commemorate this experience of David within the cave. In Psalm 142:3 David says his spirit grows faint. For those afflicted with PTSD, a sinking feeling or a rhythm change in the heart is a common sign of a panic attack. Thinking he was going to die within the cave, David felt imprisoned and it is likely his heart sunk and began to race. This is done by the PTSD mind to give the person a surge of adrenaline energy to allow them to fight or run in order to survive. Thus when David references his spirit growing faint this is likely a description of the common PTSD symptom of a panic attack. This was not the first occasion in which David was trapped, and his mind would have automatically been reminded of his close calls with death in Gath and Keilah.

In Psalm 142:4, David says no one cares about him. This supports the above observations about the PTSD mind. David indeed had low self-esteem. Although David had some of his soldiers with him in the cave, he felt as if he was alone, rejected and none of those soldiers cared about him. In reality, we know this is untrue. However within the mind of the battle-scarred David, his mind automatically assumed no one cared about him. The warrior David grew so familiar with rejection, that even in the midst of a company of faithful soldiers, he was convinced he was alone.

Moreover David viewed himself as unworthy of God's love. In Psalm 142:5-6 we see David crying out within his heart for the Lord to rescue him. David's prayers in the Psalms are often mingled with urgency. David is so convinced of his lack of worth his prayers take the form of him begging God to show him any compassion. Here the warrior pleads with God to remember him. He is so accustomed to being abandoned He always suspects God will also abandon him. However we see God's consistent faithfulness to David—even when he was forsaken by others. In this account, God delivers David from the prison of the cave. God remains ever faithful to David—even when he feels rejected by all others.

58

Dear David,

I would like to begin by challenging your statement that no one cares about you. I can understand you feel like this, but when you have these thoughts arise—confront them with truth. You have 600 men in your army who look to you for leadership—all of whom would give their lives for you. I know Abiathar the priest and Gad the prophet care about you. Although you have experienced so much rejection, there are many who love you and would put your life ahead of their own. You are loved, my dear David!

As these thoughts of negativity arise, challenge them. Tell them about the people who do love you. Tell them about the Lord God Almighty who has anointed and blessed you. Indeed God loves you, and you are altogether precious, my dear friend.

I heard you referred to yourself as a "dead dog" and a "flea." Give me opportunity to speak to you about this. If I had to pick an animal, any animal, to properly represent you, my dear David, I would pick the mightiest lion. You who are anointed from the tribe of Judah are to be the first lion in that lineage. You indeed are not a dog, or a dead dog, but a mighty cub—strong, majestic, being tested and tried in the wilderness to strengthen you for your reign upon the throne. So, my dear David, your past feelings of rejection may attempt to speak falsehood to mar your identity within your own mind, but you are indeed the first lion in the tribe of Judah. Be humble, but do not be disillusioned. You are the lion cub whom God is strengthening for the throne.

If we must select another creature with which to compare you, to dispel the thought of the "flea," then we will compare you, mighty David, to a wild bear robbed of her cubs. The wild bear who throws off all restraint to rescue her cubs from danger—the most ferocious sight in the wilderness. To your enemies you are feared because of the fire which blazes in your heart. You are most definitely not a "flea," my dear David.

Due to the rejection you have suffered in the past, you may at times imagine God will one day also reject you. Many feel unworthy of God's love. God is so good and we are so broken. My dear David, God will not

59

forsake you. He will remain with you in all your trials. You have a friend who will remain closer than a brother. Stay strong in the Lord. He will be faithful to fight for you.

Sincerely,
Genesis Pilgrim

Traumatic Experience 12: <u>Raid Campaign</u>

Read 1 Samuel 27:1-12 & Psalm 61

In this Bible passage, David and his 600 men travel to the Philistine city of Gath. After escaping from Saul another time, David is convinced the best decision is for him to leave the borders of Israel altogether. By doing so, Saul will be discouraged from continuing to pursue David.

David's arrival in Gath is different than the last time he was within this city. Previously David was arrested and brought to the Philistine city alone. Now David returns to Gath with an army of 600 loyal fighters. David was now received as a powerful military commander by Achish, the king of Gath.

This is either the same Achish to whom David was brought, or the son of the earlier Achish. Either way, the king receives David graciously and gives him a city for his troops and their families. Thus, David and his army made the city of Ziklag their home base for one year and four months.

During his stay at Ziklag, David remained independent of Achish's rule, yet he often reported to him. David led his army on various raiding missions among enemy cities. Although David was no longer living in Israel, he continued to fight against the enemies of Israel.

Similar to David's first time before Achish, king of Gath, David once again successfully uses deception to mislead the king. During his first visit to Gath, David acted insane before Achish. Now, during David's long stay in Ziklag he continually deceives Achish in all of his reports—telling him he is raiding the cities of Israel and their allies. Achish is convinced David is no longer faithful to Israel and he is pleased.

Psalm 61 was likely written to commemorate the events of 1 Samuel 27:1-12. Although Psalm 61 was written much later, after David was crowned king (Psa. 61:6), the details in the first half of this psalm reflect his time in Philistine territory. This gives us insight concerning the mind of David at this stage in his life.

Psalm 61:2 mentions David's heart feeling overwhelmed—a likely reference to a symptom of his PTSD. David feels very isolated in this foreign territory—as if he is at the ends of the earth itself (Psa. 61:2). To survive in this foreign territory, David views the Lord as his refuge and rock (Psa. 61:2-4). He views himself as surviving under the protection of the Lord's wings. This is significant because apart from God, David did not have support for himself and his men. They were surrounded by Philistine enemies. Thus, these PTSD symptoms allow David's spiritual mind to "see" God's protection all around him. This is the only way David could survive under these constant threats.

During this period, David also cried out to the Lord in prayer and made vows to Him (Psa. 61:1, 5). The lack of support in this foreign would have strengthened David's faith—compelling him to look to God for help in all potentially dangerous situations. When David was finally driven away from Israel during Saul's reign, he felt as if he was cut off from the Lord (1 Sam. 26:19). Thus, we see during this period of exile, David had an intense longing to return to the Lord's house for worship (Psa. 61:4).

Dear David,

At times we are presented with impossible situations. No matter where you travelled in Israel, Saul continued to hunt you down. Eventually he chased you away from the country altogether. Your vow of faithfulness, and refusal to harm the Lord's anointed, made it necessary for you to leave before you were forced to fight against Saul.

It must have been difficult to make the decision to leave Israel. The last time you were taken into Gath was traumatic, and it must have taken tremendous courage to choose to move into the city under your free will. It is terrifying to be surrounded by enemies. It is even more terrifying when one chooses to do this under their own volition. As you moved into Gath, thoughts must have raced through your mind about what would happen if the Philistines attempted to arrest you once again.

However, your willingness to face your fears allowed your fighters to finally have a safe home for their families in Ziklag. Thus you took your life into your hands in the hope of providing a better life for your family and the families of your men. This is a truly selfless sacrifice—which fits with your pattern of always caring for those under your command.

When stuck in difficult situations, sometimes war requires us to make the "best" decision among all bad options. As in the earlier case where you used deception to escape certain death at the hand of the Philistine king, so now you also chose to use deception. When we are surrounded by men who constantly lie to manipulate us in times of war, it is unreasonable to think we should be able to maintain absolute honesty.

In times of war, survival of your people comes first. At times we are put in difficult situations and must do the best we can to maintain our integrity. However, at the core of all warfare is the art of deception. Any successful commander must make his strengths appear as weaknesses, and his weaknesses appear as strength. The successful commander must deceive the enemy into thinking he is moving when he is still, and still while he is moving. Thus within warfare, deception is absolutely critical, and all warfare is based on deception (Sun Tzu, Art of War).

So I do not see your use of deception as a moral flaw. Instead, your use of deception is a common practice used by all successful commanders. All men of God who are called to serve in combat struggle with this principle of warfare. However, deception is required in all applications of military force. I trust you will be encouraged in my words here, David. Survive first. Then take care to leave behind you the methods of the battlefield when you find yourself in safety.

The rules of the battlefield are not compatible with the rules of the citizenry. Let your battle-scarred mind lead you to survival in war, but once you find yourself in peace allow this portion of your brain to rest peacefully until you recall it into service. Until next time, my dear David.

Sincerely,
Genesis Pilgrim

Traumatic Experience 13: <u>Compelled Participation in Philistine March against Israel</u>

Read 1 Samuel 29:1-11 & Psalm 58

Earlier we read King Achish of Gath allowed David to stay in Ziklag. During the next year and four months, David's army and all their families remained in the city as their home base. As a part of David's deal with King Achish, David agreed to be the bodyguard of the king (1 Sam. 28:1-2).

This was a good deal for both Achish and David. Achish received the allegiance of the powerful war commander, David, and 600 additional soldiers to fight for him if ever Gath marched to war. David received a location where the families of his army could dwell in safety, in addition to David finally being free of Saul's pursuits. David was correct: Saul never attempted to move into Philistine territory to capture David.

However, David's vow to serve as the bodyguard of King Achish turned out to have nearly disastrous consequences. The Philistines decided to march to war against Israel. Now David was forced into a terrible position: David was required to march to war against Israel.

We can imagine the inner conflict this would have caused within David. Earlier when repeatedly threatened by King Saul, David refused to raise a hand against the Lord's anointed. David would not harm Saul and vowed to never do so. Now in a twist of fate, David was ordered by his new king to march to war against King Saul.

David was indeed within a dilemma—a most impossible situation. He could not refuse the order of King Achish, nor could David harm King Saul. Moreover, Israel as a nation was also "anointed" by the Lord as His people, so neither could David raise a weapon against his own Israelite countrymen.

Thus, David set out on the battle march with King Achish in deception. David told Achish he would fight against Israel. However, David knew in his heart he would not raise a weapon in the battle due to his earlier vows to never harm Saul.

David's army set out within the Philistine battle procession. During this time, David's heart must have raced as he attempted to think of a way out of this situation. Ultimately as in all difficult situations, David would have trusted in the Lord to somehow deliver him.

As he marched on, the Lord allowed dissent among the Philistine military commanders as an answer to David's prayer. The Philistine commanders doubted David's faithfulness to their nation. As a result, the Philistine commanders asked King Achish to dismiss David and his army. In this way, God arranged circumstances to allow David to remain true to his vow: He would not raise a hand against the Lord's anointed.

In 1 Sam. 29:6, King Achish uses the phrase, "as surely as the Lord lives." When speaking with David, this Philistine king mentions the God of David. We are left to consider why the Philistine would have referred to the God of Israel. It is possible he did this simply out of respect for David. Or the Philistine king could have seen the usefulness of the Lord as a "god" who can grant victory in battle. Since the Philistines were marching to war, Achish could have desired help from the same God who gave David such incredible military prowess.

Either way, we know the testimony of David had an impact for good upon Achish. David was a living testimony of the ability of his God to preserve him in all battles. And in this time of war, King Achish needed the strongest "god" to be on his side. So during this moment of crisis Achish could be appealing to the Lord rather than trusting in the relatively unproven "gods" of the Philistines. Although Achish is sending David away, he desires for David to leave with him the favor of his God.

Perhaps this plays a part in ensuring Philistine success in the upcoming battle. Whereas the Philistine king appeals to the Lord God; King Saul finally appeals to the witch at Endor for help. As the two forces meet in battle with David absent, the favor of the Lord rests upon the Philistine army. Israel is defeated, with both Saul and Jonathan dying on the battlefield.

Psalm 58 was *possibly* written to commemorate the events of this Bible passage. In 1 Samuel 29:2-4, David reacts to the rejection offered to him from the Philistine rulers who dissuaded King Achish from bringing David into the battle (Psa. 58:1-10). Rejection is hard to accept—regardless of the circumstances. Regardless of what David would have chosen to do in the battle, it was nonetheless stinging for him to endure deriding comments from the Philistine rulers who pre-judged him as a traitor.

Although David's loyalty to Achish was likely feigned, it still was not easy for him to accept rejection (1 Sam. 29:8). David was in an impossible place. He was rejected by King Saul and compelled to leave Israel. Now he was rejected by the Philistines and discharged from their army while marching on the road during a deployment. This may be why the emotions evoked in Psalm 58 are so intense. David asks for God's total judgment on these Philistine rulers (Psa. 58:6-9).

The psalm concludes with David's appeal to the Lord as the Judge of the entire earth (Psa. 58:10-11). This could fit within this context as David asked God to preside over the battle between Israel and the Philistines. David was dismissed from both Israel and the Philistines. Since David could no longer participate in the battle on either side, he asks God to enter into the battle to reward the righteous and punish the wicked.

Dear David,

It is good to hear you were delivered from trouble. The Lord put within the minds of the Philistine rulers to ask you to leave the battle march. I am convinced of this. This allowed you to stay true to your vow not to harm Saul.

When we are stuck and see no way out, we can rely on the Lord to make a way for us. Many times you were trapped. Many times it appeared as if you were beyond hope. Yet the Lord continues to pull you away from the grasp of the grave. This occasion was no different than all the other times in which the Lord delivered you.

However in this case, you had to merely pray and wait. Your own hand or persuasion did not earn your deliverance. Instead, God moved to accomplish this ahead of you—convincing the Philistine rulers to order your discharge from the battle march.

I am reminded of the earlier way in which God first delivered you as you fled from Saul. As Saul and his men pursued you, the Holy Spirit came upon them—forcing them to stop their pursuit as they prophesied. God personally disrupted Saul from catching up with you. Now it seems God is doing something similar. As an answer to prayer he confounds the minds of those who plan to lead you into harm's way.

Overall, we can be sure God is faithful. At times, all we are required to do is to stand. Stand fast in faith and wait for God's deliverance. Remember: The battle belongs to the Lord. He will safeguard you as you wait patiently upon him. Until next time, David.

Sincerely,
Genesis Pilgrim

Traumatic Experience 14: <u>Amalekite Battle to Rescue Captured Families</u>

Read 1 Samuel 30:1-25

In this Bible passage, David and his army of 600 men return to Ziklag after being discharged from the Philistine battle march. When arriving at their home city, they discover an Amalekite raiding army burned their city and captured their family members. Immediately, David and his army mourn until they have no strength left.

At this point, none of the men would have known what was happening to their family members. Some of the soldiers blamed David and began to plot to kill him for allowing this to happen.

In this time of distress, David turns to the priest, Abiathar. The two pray together for the Lord's guidance. Although the army was exhausted from the three day journey they just completed, God directed David to lead them in pursuit of the Amalekite army.

Although 200 of David's men were too exhausted to continue, David and the remaining 400 caught the Amalekites. They fought them for nearly 24 hours before the last group of Amalekites fled. Thus, David recovered all of the captured family members.

When returning from the battle, some of David's soldiers plotted against the 200 that remained behind—suggesting the 200 did not deserve any of the plunder. David responded by saying all his soldiers would have an equal share—regardless of whether they fought or remained behind.

When considering the typically negative pattern of events in his life, it is fitting David would be thrust within a new tragedy after his discharge from King Achish's military. David experienced a close call in the previous event—narrowly escaping being pulled into a war against Israel. David immediately experiences another tragedy by discovering the destruction of his home base in Ziklag.

This stacking of tragic events is common in David's life: For example, he had a sheep that was attacked by a lion, then a sheep attacked by a bear (1 Sam. 17:34-36). He eludes capture from Saul, but then is captured by the Philistines (1 Sam. 19:9-21:15). Battles also blur together due to their frequency (1 Sam. 18:30).

The stacking of tragedy is significant in David's mind. By being unable to fully process events before being thrown into further tragedy, David's mind is constantly left reeling between past and present events. This contributes to the development of PTSD, with symptoms arising from the mind's attempt to properly deal with each emerging trauma based on past experiences. Being unable to grieve and come to grips with past events puts the mind into a constant defensive state. The mind develops PTSD as a coping strategy to help the person adjust immediately to emerging crises.

When experiencing the aftermath of a tragedy, it is important to allow the mind time to process the event. Grieving and understanding one's emotions is important. Often the events of a tragedy occur so quickly they blur together. By revisiting the experience with a counselor, the person is able to match each emotion to each scene of the tragedy through "cognitive processing therapy" (CPT). This helps the person to organize their emotions. If this is accomplished, the person has a chance of avoiding the runaway emotional patterns which may develop if left untreated.

Clearly, the continuous series of tragedies experienced by David did not allow him to come to grips with his experiences. As a result, David's writing in the Psalms shows mental patterns typical of a warrior with PTSD. He imagines rejection and betrayal everywhere. David imagines God will reject him in one moment, and in the next he trusts in God as his refuge. He has a powerful ability to transport himself from his surroundings, being able to visualize God as a fortress surrounding him.

This PTSD symptom is called derealization. The person with PTSD is so accustomed to trauma they can learn to look to the supernatural for security. To some level all people of faith need to have this ability. To frame one's mind on the spiritual reality which cannot be physically seen requires the ability to dissociate from one's surroundings. In other words, one's relationship with God is the product of experienced trauma, or a learned behavior stemming from someone else's trauma. The person of faith uses trauma to assist their minds in forming thoughts of spiritual security.

70

This is why David often talks about the Lord as a refuge, fortress and stronghold. It is also why the Lord Jesus says the kingdom of heaven is within or near each believer (Luke 17:21). Experiencing the kingdom of God is something which occurs as our minds are touched by the Holy Spirit. Thus, a believer sees and experiences the kingdom within and around them now. Therefore, faith itself is dissociation from the physical world. All faith can be traced to trauma—whether experienced firsthand or taught through the trauma of another.

Dear David,

At times we do not have the opportunity to properly understand a tragic event before something else happens. It seems from what you tell me you often face one difficult situation after another. This makes it nearly impossible to find healing from these experiences, and also leads to confusion within our minds.

This is a common occurrence among warriors like you. When we are not given time to grieve and to mentally process events our minds are left reeling. Over time we develop intense emotions that seem to have minds of their own. Rather than emotions being the result of a direct experience, our emotions can be incongruent with our physical surroundings. Our PTSD mind can give us intense surges of emotions which do not fit our current surroundings. Here is my advice for these moments . . .

(1) Since your mind is so powerful to imagine and bring on intense emotions, use this in your relationship with God. Do not allow the negative aspects of this gift to overwhelm you, dear David. Rather, when your mind gives you intense emotions, direct them toward God. Cry out to Him in your heart. See the spiritual fortress around you—providing you with divine protection. The PTSD mind can be viewed as a disability, but it can also be viewed as a beneficial attribute granting you deeper spirituality. Your mind's ability to respond to "unseen danger" can also be used to great purpose to sense "unseen protection" from the Lord God Almighty.

(2) Rely upon others to check your emotions. When you feel a surge of emotions, when your heart begins to race and when your vision tightens, look to those around you. Keep the priest, Abiathar, and other faithful counselors near to you during all your travels, my dear David. When your mind races, confess it to them and pray with them. They can help you to determine if your rising anxiety fits your situation. Then they can help you to direct those intense emotions to the Lord. You will see, my dear David, the scars you bear from war can be used to great benefit in helping you to rely on God.

(3) When your intense emotions do not fit your physical surroundings, consider this: God may be leading you to respond to an

unseen spiritual reality moving around you. His Spirit is communicating with your mind. At those moments you feel your heart racing and your anxiety rising for no reason, this should be seen as the Holy Spirit calling you to prayer. These feelings may be your sensing of the angelic kingdom around you. Use these moments to their maximum spiritual benefit—see the supernatural fortress of God and allow yourself to be revitalized with power from beyond the curtain of this world. If at all possible, call for the priest and spend moments in prayer with him when you are so prompted.

My dear David, my heart goes out to you. As you put this advice into practice you will grow much in your relationship with the Lord. You will find your "disability" is indeed a spiritual ability—a gift from God allowing you to readily interact with the Holy Spirit.

As you have seen in your latest struggle, this spiritual fortress can be relied upon for a source of strength when we are physically exhausted. When we have nothing left to give physically, we can shift our minds to the spiritual, re-charge in a moment, and then bring that strength into our physical surroundings. I trust this provided you the ability to press on in your pursuit of the Amalekites even though you were already exhausted.

Although very difficult to master, we can look to the spiritual fortress of the Lord to give us peace in the midst of betrayals. I was especially pleased to see how you masterfully put aside the bickering of the 400 men against the 200. God is giving you wisdom. Thus when you are called to give an account before an assembly do not consider your answer ahead of time. Ever trust on the Spirit to give you the right answer for the moment. In these things you will be blessed, my dead David.

Sincerely,
Genesis Pilgrim

Traumatic Experience 15: Death of Saul and Jonathan

Read 2 Samuel 1:1-27 & Psalm 4

King Saul and Jonathan perished in Israel's battle with the Philistines. This was the same battle to which David marched with the Philistines under the command of King Achish of Gath. However, due to being discharged, David and his army of 600 did not participate in the battle. Later David, hears of the deaths of Jonathan and King Saul. In this Bible passage, David mourns the deaths of these two men.

When David hears the report of Saul's death, he learns another man assisted Saul in completing his suicide attempt. David orders the execution of the man—perhaps because his story seemed fishy. There was no way to validate from another person if what he reported was true. David faulted the man for making the decision to kill Saul, rather than attempting to place him on a horse and rush him off the battlefield. There may have been hope to rescue Saul and somehow nurse him back to health. Saul may have died after his rescue, but all possible effort should have been made.

Saul was "anointed" by the Lord—which placed him in the succession of the Judges, who were entrusted by the Spirit with the mission of saving Israel. To kill an "anointed" judge, regardless of his likelihood for survival, is to be unconcerned with the deliverance of the entire nation of Israel. So when the man raised his hand against Saul, the king in the lineage of the Judges, the man may have caused a crime which would somehow rob the nation of a future deliverance through Saul.

In this passage, David's mourning for Jonathan and Saul represent a major turning point. Prior to this event, traumatic events occur in David's life with minimal reflection and nearly no time taken for mourning. However, in this Bible passage, David makes a deliberate effort to remember the fallen.

When dealing with the aftermath of trauma, it is important a person allows time for grief. This is why funerals are necessary. A person needs to carefully consider what happened to the person who was lost and how their life was touched by the deceased. This process may time a lot of time, but it is necessary to help the person to mentally categorize the trauma within their worldview.

For example, if the person "felt they were unloved" by the deceased, then attending a funeral will provide the data their mind needs to either confirm or dispel that belief. The person can attend the funeral and listen to stories of the deceased. This helps their mind make subconscious connections to their own relationship with the deceased. This may lead one to the subconscious conclusion that the deceased did in fact love them, but perhaps had a difficult time expressing it.

Thus, taking the time to grieve and mourn is necessary for all survivors. Mourning assists the mind in properly framing intense emotions through the subjective stories told by others. However, if mourning is not allowed its proper place, the emotions of the survivor tend to grow and distort over time—giving rise to increased disillusionment.

As we view David's process of mourning for Jonathan and Saul, we see he had a breakthrough. David tears his clothes—signifying to everyone who would see him that he was mourning. To channel his emotions, David writes a poem about the deceased. This helps David to build a truthful picture of where these men fit within society and how his life was touched by them.

In the poem, David reshapes his own identity. He places himself within Israel by deriding the Philistines who killed Jonathan (2 Sam. 1:20). After being chased out of Israel by Saul, David needed to mourn to mentally find his place back within the nation. Thus mourning helped David to remember the long lost reality: He was not a bodyguard for King Achish. He did not belong to the Philistines. He was not rejected by his people Israel—but was a part of them. David's poem helps him to place himself within the nation once again—for the first time after he fled from Saul many years earlier.

Although David was greatly mistreated by Saul, David's poem helps him reframe his mind on Saul's true identity. Saul was a great leader of Israel. He was responsible for its deliverance. This is how David "chooses" to remember Saul (2 Sam. 1:21-24). Therefore, mourning allows David to reframe years of trauma caused by being pursued by Saul. Although the effects of the trauma may linger in David's PTSD, mourning here allows David to forgive Saul. David might not have control of his past, but he does have the ability to determine how those events will affect him in the future. Thus, David chooses to remember Saul fondly in his final tribute.

The poem concludes with David's lament of Jonathan—saying the love of Jonathan was better than the love of women. How is this so? When considering David often feared betrayal in social settings, Jonathan never betrayed David. Even under pressure from his father, Jonathan never turned his back on David. This represents the closest of friendships.

Throughout David's life he constantly struggles in social settings—imagining those around him of plotting against him. David felt rejection from his own parents and from his own brothers. Overall, the faithfulness of Jonathan represented something powerful to David: People can be trusted.

This memory of Jonathan's faithfulness will continue to bear fruit in David's life. It will inspire him to trust people on occasion, but most importantly it serves as perhaps the only perfect picture in his life of God's faithfulness. Jonathan had nothing to gain by being faithful to David, yet he did it anyway. This is the picture of God's love for David. Since Jonathan remained "always faithful" to David, this meant David could truly trust God to remain "always faithful" as well. This is how the mere presence of Jonathan helped David to find strength in the Lord (1 Sam. 23:16). Thus, mourning Jonathan helps David's mind to capture this reality.

Psalm 4 may commemorate David's feelings at this stage in his life. In Psalm 4, David discusses his condition of emotional distress (Psa. 4:1). At this time, David was still in exile due to the lies propagated by King Saul. Now that Saul is deceased, David rhetorically asks his people if they will continue to shame him, or if they will finally recognize the Lord is with him as their anointed ruler (Psa. 4:2-3).

The people have a major decision ahead of them—who indeed will they select to rule now that Saul is slain? Which man has the ability to lead the nation into prosperity (Psa. 4:6)? David urges his people to search their hearts silently, trusting in the Lord to arrive at the best decision (Psa. 4:4-5). Confident he will be called forth as the king of Judah, David rests in peace (Psa. 4:7-8). Whereas the people are in turmoil, wondering what to do next, David is confident of the Lord's protection—having faith in the anointing he received as a boy from the prophet Samuel.

Dear David,

I am saddened for your loss. I am encouraged, however, that you had opportunity to grieve.

I love your poem! When we are gripped by grief it is so hard to find the right words to speak, but writing gives us the ability to search for just the right words. Your poem is beautiful. I enjoy how you paint a picture with your writing. Writing is a great outlet, and the Lord has given you skill in it. Please write more when you have time. I am convinced there are many who could find encouragement in it.

Previously we discussed the importance of mourning when we experience loss. I am thankful you took the precious time to mourn. Our minds need to have opportunity to sort through traumatic events. I can see your poem is helping your mind to be healthier.

In your poem you discussed the Philistines as being separate from you. Although you have lived in Ziklag for one year and four months, you can make the choice now to close that chapter in your life. You can choose to embrace your identity within Israel. There is nothing to hinder you from making this change now. You might have stayed with the Philistines for a while, but close that chapter in your life, dear David.

In every generation, the Lord raises up leaders (whether Judges or Kings) to deliver His people. Remember the anointing that has been placed upon you. Allow yourself to grieve, but as the time for grieving passes, accept your mission from the Lord as the next Judge/King in a long lineage of deliverers. God will be faithful to work through you to shepherd his people.

The task of being a national leader is overwhelming, but continue to look to the Lord for leadership and you will be blessed. Surround yourself with faithful, skilled men who can advise and serve you.

I look forward to our next meeting.

Sincerely,

Genesis Pilgrim

Traumatic Experience 16: <u>Jebusite Battle at Jerusalem</u>

Read 2 Samuel 3:27-39; 4:5-12; 5:1-10 & Psalms 2, 23, 108

After the death of Jonathan and Saul, David travelled to the city of Hebron. David was anointed as the King of Judah. Israel remained faithful to the house of Saul and placed one of Saul's descendants on the throne. Judah and Israel were at war with one another for 7 years and 6 months. David remained somewhat neutral during this period as the generals of the two nations waged battles against one another.

In 2 Samuel 3:27-39, Judah's army general, Joab, assassinated Abner, the general of Israel. David properly mourns the loss of Abner. David declares himself innocent of Abner's death and places blame on Joab. David tears his clothes, fasts and puts on sackcloth. Then he walks in the funeral procession. At the burial location, David weeps aloud in front of the people and sings a funeral song. In this, David becomes even more proficient in mourning than he was at the deaths of Jonathan and Saul.

Mourning is a necessary part of healing. Earlier after the deaths of the priests at Nob, David accepts blame for the deaths of the priests due to his inability to cope through a funeral (1 Sam. 22:22). However, at the funeral of Abner, David subconsciously labels his emotions within his mind. David is clear in pointing out he did not intend the death of Abner and did not commit it. Thus, attending Abner's funeral absolved David from developing a false self-perception later on. Joab murdered Abner, just as Doeg murdered the priests. David is not responsible for either loss.

In 2 Samuel 4:5-12, two evil men assassinate the king of Israel. When the assassins report the death to King David in Judah, he orders them executed. The two assassins believed they would be rewarded by King David, yet he would not be partner with them in their crime. He distanced himself from their crime by having them put to death.

Then Israel asked David to serve as king of their nation. David agreed and was appointed as king over both Judah and Israel. David was thirty years old (2 Sam. 5:4).

The anointing of David as the king of Israel is followed by a battle with the Jebusites. In 2 Samuel 5:6, King David leads his people to fight against the Jebusite city of Jerusalem. David captures the city and establishes it as his new capital. David lives within the fortress and it is called the "City of David."

Psalm 108 may have been written to commemorate David's ascension to Jerusalem. In this psalm, David mentions the different regions of Israel and Judah—which were now combined under his reign as king over the two nations. He explains that the Lord no longer goes out with Israel's armies—which would be the sentiment due to the deaths of Jonathan and Saul years earlier in battle (Psa.108:11). Moreover Israel and Judah experienced civil war for years after the death of Saul, so they did not war with foreign nations during this time. Last, the psalm mentions being led up to the fortified city—which may apply to Jerusalem itself (Psa. 108:10).

After many years in the wilderness, being compelled to look to the Lord as his spiritual fortress, David now takes up residence within a physical fortress. This might not have been a good step for David, as it is likely being within the fortress may have given him random flashbacks to unfavorable experiences within fortresses. Earlier in his life, David was arrested and brought to King Achish in the fortress of Gath—where he feared for his life. Then David was nearly captured by Saul within the gated city of Keilah. David was also nearly captured when he was trapped within a cave. Now, David lives within a physical fortress where he actually fought a battle.

We are left to consider if David had flashbacks of those previous close calls while residing in the fortress. Many of David's psalms discuss the feelings of being trapped in similar situations, as previously demonstrated in "Traumatic Experiences 5, 6, 9 & 11" above. Thus, as David lived within the fortified city of Jerusalem, he may have received flashbacks to those moments where he was trapped in such places—which led to him penning these psalms. Although David was "safe" in Jerusalem, his mind would not allow him to enjoy it. As he looks within his courts,

David ever imagines people are plotting against him. Thus, David's mind imports a battle within the walls of the fortress.

Psalm 23 was likely written to commemorate this period in David's life. In Psalm 23:1-3, David reflects on the rest provided by the Lord. For the first time in his life, within his own fortress, David may at times feel at peace. When he is drawn into PTSD panic attacks as his mind races to past battlefields, David prayerfully brings his mind to the realization that the Lord Himself is his deliverer (Psa. 23:4). Although Israel is still surrounded by enemies who David will fight in future chapters, for the moment he has a table set before him where he can experience God's bounty (Psa. 23:5). He concludes this psalm with a focus upon dwelling in the Lord's house (Psa. 23:6). Thus, it is no surprise David makes immediate plans to transport the ark of the Lord to Jerusalem (2 Sam. 6:1-2).

In Acts 4:25, it states Psalm 2 was written by David. In this psalm, David commemorates the experiences of this Bible passage. He mentions the placement of Israel's king in Zion—which was completed with David's victory over Jerusalem (Psa. 2:6). In Psalm 2:1-3, the upcoming plotting of the nations around Israel is reflected. Last, in verses 10-12 we see the Lord plans to give Israel victory over those enemies. Ultimately all of these things take place in the following chapters of 2 Samuel.

Moreover, Psalm 2:12 shows us the short fuse of David. Referring to himself, David states his wrath can flare up in a moment. This is a common symptom of PTSD—as the individual displays irritability, aggression, heightened startle reaction and resulting emotional distress that is incongruent with their surroundings.

The short fuse of Psalm 2:12 also applies to the Lord Himself as a messianic prophecy. Certainly, the cleansings of the temple would support this (John 2:14-16). Thus, in the expression of David's emotions he actually feels the same intensity felt by the Lord Jesus.

Dear David,

Your recent experiences show kings are not safe within fortresses. The assassination of the king and the general you just experienced show that rulers are often subject to plots.

It is great to hear Israel's civil war with Judah has ended. The people of the Lord should not war among themselves, especially when surrounded by enemies.

Now that you have taken up residence within the fortress of Jerusalem, turn your attention to the deliverance of Israel from all their enemies. You were anointed for the purpose of delivering your people. God will give you wisdom to complete the journey ahead.

Now that you are king, you will have opportunity to accomplish all your heart desires. As you consider your next steps, I recommend you look back to the very beginning—when you were anointed. Much has passed since then, so it may be easy to lose sight of why you were called.

Recently you wrote a psalm I think captures your heart when you were anointed (Psa. 27). In it you say that even though your father and you mother have forsaken you, the Lord will receive you. At the very beginning, you turned to the Lord as your Father—trusting him to care for you during your feelings of abandonment.

Over your many difficult years (from teenager to age 30), the Lord has been faithful to you as a Father. He has delivered you from all harm. He allowed you to be disciplined by difficult times, yet remained by your side to serve as your faithful Father for every experience.

Indeed, your life is a monument to the Lord's faithfulness. You rescue the downtrodden, just as you rescued your sheep. This is a reflection of what the Lord has done for you by becoming your loving Father.

When considering the next step for your kingship, commemorate this. These thoughts will provide hope and encouragement to those who also feel rejected by their families and society. If you focus on honoring the Lord, this will give all people who are experiencing difficult times like you an opportunity to look to the Lord God for help during their difficult times.

I will pray for you during this time as you plan your next steps. What an exciting time! The Lord will give you wisdom and strength.
    Sincerely,
    Genesis Pilgrim

Traumatic Experience 17: <u>Two Philistine Battles</u>

Read 2 Samuel 5:17-25 & Psalms 26, 144

During the seven years David was king of Judah, Israel was at civil war with Judah. This may explain why the Philistines apparently stopped fighting Israel during this period following the death of King Saul. King Achish and the other rulers may have still viewed David as one of their allies. And this would have appeared to be the case due to David's nation (Judah) fighting Israel.

Earlier when fleeing from Saul, David stayed with the Philistine king, Achish. However, when David is named king of Israel this seems like the greatest betrayal to the Philistines. David, the military commander who once swore fealty to Achish, is now the king of Israel. Thus, David's acceptance of the Israelite throne was met with an immediate response from the Philistines.

Following David's appointment to the throne of Israel, the Philistines might have felt duped. This would explain why the Philistines immediately decided to attack David in this Bible passage.

The Philistines marched nearly all the way to Jerusalem—stopping at the Valley of Rephaim between Bethlehem and the capital. David prays for guidance and the Lord directs him to fight the Philistines. During their defeat, the Philistines left behind their idols. Then, David issues orders to burn all the Philistine "gods" (1 Chr. 14:12).

Later, the Philistines returned to the Valley of Rephaim to challenge Israel in battle. David again prays for guidance, and the Lord gives him specific instructions. David is commanded to move his forces to the rear of the Philistine army. Then the Lord tells David he must wait for a specific signal in the movement of the trees before he begins his assault. The Philistines fled the battle, and David's forces chased them all the way to Gezer—nearly 20 miles west.

In Psalm 144 there are several clues concerning David's thoughts at this stage of his life. As David realized Israel was surrounded by enemy nations, he asks God for two things. First, David asks God to give him strength and skill for the upcoming battles (Psa. 144:1, 10-11). Second, realizing that God's supernatural action against the Philistines was instrumental in the victory, he asks him to continue granting His help to Israel (2 Sam. 5:20-24 & Psa.144:5-7).

David predicts God will give him the victory over many nations as He brings them under his power (Psa. 144:2). The goal of David is to usher his nation into a period of peace and prosperity—where social and agricultural growth continues uninterrupted (Psa. 144:12-15). This is fulfilled during the reign of David's son, Solomon.

Psalm 26 was likely written to commemorate this Bible passage. Following his victories over the Philistines, David has opportunity for reflection within his Jerusalem fortress. David is inspired to move the ark into Jerusalem as the crowning adornment of God's presence in the Lord's house in Zion.

At this stage, David views his life as blameless within his generation. Indeed this was before the incident with Bathsheba and Uriah, so it makes sense that David may still have such a high self-appraisal (Psa. 26:1-8, 11-12). This high self-appraisal serves as a key motivating factor to inspire him to move the ark in 2 Samuel 6. The high self-appraisal precedes David's assumption of his liturgical role as a community worship leader. Within this stage, leading up to 2 Samuel 6 and after it, David moves into a role as a religious leader.

Seeing Psalms, where David's writing focuses simply on teaching people to "see" God, may also be associated with this period in David's life before and after the transportation of the ark to Jerusalem. This may be why certain psalms, such as Psalm 15, 24, 29, 65, 70, 72, 95, 103, 122, 131, 133, 145, focus on providing teaching without the inclusion of many PTSD symptoms which often characterize David's other psalms. During this stage and extending to the end of his life, David was focused on serving as a liturgical leader of Israel, so the Seeing Psalms are focused on the exclusive goal of teaching people to "see" God for themselves; not his typical candid, emotional venting found in his other psalms.

In other words, from this point on, when David is having a "good" day, he thinks like a liturgical leader and feels the "mountain top" experiences of the Seeing Psalms. But on "bad" days where David struggles with his PTSD, he is consumed by the symptoms associated with the Symptom Psalms. (David's "Symptom Psalms" will be discussed in Section 2 & David's "Seeing Psalms" will be discussed in Section 3.)

Dear David,

It is great that Israel and Judah are no longer at war with one another. This means you can unite them in some common goals. Rather than the two nations being harassed separately by neighboring nations, you can use your kingship to lead all the people in battle.

Remember your anointing. Just as the Judges, you have been anointed and indwelled by the Spirit of the Lord for a specific purpose—to rescue God's people. God will give you strength and courage for each task which lies before you.

Do not become overwhelmed by the many nations who stand opposed to you. Simply fight the battles the Lord places before you on each day. Trust the Lord to battle for you.

It is encouraging to see the Lord came to your rescue on the battlefield in your two wars with the Philistines. Just as Israel trusted in the Angel of the Lord to go before them into the Promised Land, you can now trust the Angel of the Lord to care for you. Look to the Lord like the leaders of Israel's past—Moses, Joshua and the Judges.

As you reflect on the history of Israel, make it a part of your daily routine to have the Law read in your presence. This will give you wisdom in the days to come. You will find the people will look to you for religious instruction just as they looked to Moses.

Take care to provide lessons to inspire the nation you lead. Write them down and have them read within the congregation. You are brave. You have survived so many traumatic experiences. I am confident your thoughts can provide encouragement to others who have difficult times ahead of them. When you write down your thoughts, take care to record those thoughts which may serve to encourage others. In this you will be greatly blessed, my dear David.

> *Sincerely,*
> *Genesis Pilgrim*

Traumatic Experience 18: <u>Death of Uzzah</u>

Read 2 Samuel 6:1-19 & Psalms 30, 40

In this Bible passage, David chooses to move the ark of God into Jerusalem. This is done with much rejoicing. Thirty thousand people were present to offer praise as the ark was moved.

However, David does not follow the specific instructions in the Law of Moses (Exo. 25:14-15). Rather than the ark being carried by poles, it is moved by cart. Much earlier, after the Philistines captured the ark, they also transported it by cart (1 Sam. 6:7-8). The Lord afflicted the Philistines for their irreverent treatment of the ark. Likewise, the Lord strikes Uzzah, the priest, and he dies.

Then the Bible says David was angry (2 Sam. 6:8). But, the Bible does not tell us the subject to whom David's anger was directed. Perhaps David was angry at many. David could have been angry at himself for overlooking the command to carry the ark with poles (Exo. 25:14-15). David could have been angry at the priests and his advisers in failing to advise him on the proper transport of the ark. He may have also been angry at Uzzah for reaching out, or angry at the driver of the cart. Or he might have been angry at the oxen for stumbling. Regardless of the subject of David's anger, it resulted in him fearing God and refusing to move the ark further (2 Sam 6:9-10).

Three months later, David chose to re-attempt movement of the ark. Similar to the first attempt, the movement of the ark was accompanied with praise. During this attempt, however, the ark is moved by poles—in accordance with the Law of Moses. After six steps were taken, a sacrifice was performed. As the people danced, the ark continued until it arrived at its place within the tabernacle in the City of David. Then David offered burnt offerings and fellowship offerings. After blessing all the people, David gave them food—loaves of bread, raisin cakes and date cakes.

However, this great time of joy was also met with heartache. David's wife, Michal, criticized David for his worship. Rather than participating in the event, she chose to look down upon him from a window.

The introduction of Psalm 30 states it was written for the dedication of the temple. However, the temple was not constructed until the reign of King Solomon. Thus, Psalm 30 may have been written to commemorate this event where David set up the tabernacle and the ark of God within Jerusalem.

In Psalm 30:3, David says God saved him from death during all his travels. As a result, David explains he is moved to joyful dancing (Psa. 30:11-12). Certainly this description within Psalm 30 fits the events of 2 Samuel 6:1-19. David reasons that, because God has allowed him to keep within him the breath of life, he would use his breath to loudly praise the Lord (Psa. 30:9).

Psalm 40 may have also been written to commemorate the events of 2 Samuel 6. Psalm 40:6-10 mentions David speaking before the great assembly, in addition to the offering of sacrifices—which would fit the occasion of this Bible passage (2 Sam. 6:17-18). Moreover, in Psalm 40:12-14, David states he has many troubles and those who desire to take his life. This time of distress would fit the national circumstances surrounding 2 Samuel 6. Israel recently completed two battles with the Philistines, and soon they will be called to war against the Moabites, Arameans, Ammonites and Edomites.

Indeed these enemy armies could be the troubles faced by David in Psalm 40:12-14. Although the arrival of the ark within Jerusalem marked a time of great rejoicing, it was also at a time of national crisis—as Israel was surrounded by enemies who all worked diligently to remove David from his throne.

In Psalm 40:12, David experiences emotional distress as his grief causes his heart to feel as if it is failing. Among those with PTSD, heart disorders, such as atrial fibrillation, can occur. Panic attacks can cause pattern disruptions within the heart. It is likely the failure of David's heart is a description of the sinking and racing heart symptoms which often accompany panic attacks.

Dear David,

I am sorry for your loss of Uzzah. He dedicated his life to the Lord—serving him as a priest. And in his passing he closed his eyes in the carrying out of his service to the Lord. Although his death was unexpected, he will be remembered. His passing signifies a major change in Israel's history as the ark of God's might was brought within the capital.

At times of loss, we can feel rushes of emotion. It is good you feel anger. Never forget you have many people who love you, David. Many times a warrior is self-convinced they must be grave—fighting back emotion as they fight back enemy troops. When feeling conflicted by your emotions, do not force them back. Rather, confide this to your prophet, Nathan, or your priest, Abiathar. They can pray with you, helping you to work through your thoughts one step at a time.

It is good to hear you are establishing Jerusalem as a great location for Israel. The presence of the Lord's house and the ark in Jerusalem will remind the people that the Lord is the true King of the people. Your desire to place the Lord's house near your palace will serve to keep people mindful of this for many generations: The Lord is the great King of the nation.

It can be overwhelming—considering the many enemy nations around Israel. Indeed, only about seven years ago, King Saul fell in battle against the Philistines. However, when you feel overwhelmed and your heart begins to race, remember how the Lord delivered the Philistines into your hand. You can trust the Lord to go out with your army in future battles. Never lose sight of this faith which has the power to quiet your heart and sustain you, my dear David.

Master your own heart. When it races it is trying to bring something to your attention. Receive the report it offers you. Then provide it comfort. Tell your heart it can rest securely as you develop a good plan to address whatever problem it brought to mind. Ask the Lord to stand watch for your heart. This will allow you to sleep securely—trusting God to watch over you during times where you are physically vulnerable.
    Sincerely,
    Genesis Pilgrim

Traumatic Experience 19: <u>War with Philistines, Moabites, Arameans and Edomites</u>

Read 2 Samuel 8:1-14 & Psalms 25, 60

In this Bible passage, David leads Israel into war against various enemies, in the following order: the Philistines, Moabites, Arameans and Edomites. With David as the newly appointed leader of Israel, these nations sought to topple David before he could build momentum for his people. In other words, these nations moved quickly in an attempt to stop Israel from becoming a regional super power.

Earlier, the Philistines humbled Israel when King Saul and Jonathan were slain upon the battlefield. Now that Israel once again has a powerful warrior-king, these nations sought to kill David before he could fully rebuild the nation. However, this would be a failed effort as the Lord God would ensure David's success on all battlefields.

First, in 2 Samuel 8:1, David soundly defeats the Philistines. In the earlier two battles, the Philistines marched near Jerusalem to threaten David close to his own fortress (2 Sam. 5:1-21). But, in this battle, David takes the fight to the Philistines—pushing deep within their territory to capture the chief Philistine city of Gath (1 Chr. 18:1). Holding key regions of the Philistines would have provided a buffer zone to protect Israel. This would reduce the likelihood of Philistines being able to penetrate far into Israelite territory as they had done previously.

This is the ultimate victory. David now captures the city of Gath—where he once stood as a prisoner before King Achish (1 Sam. 21:10-15; Psa. 56). This city of Gath was also where David was compelled to feign allegiance to the Philistine king for one year and four months (1 Sam. 27:1-12). Now David wrests this city of great importance from the Philistines and thus grants remedy to the wrongs he suffered within it.

Second, in 2 Samuel 8:2, David defeated the Moabites. After the battle, David orders the execution of two-thirds of the Moabites. One-third is permitted to live under the agreement they will serve David. This execution ensured Moab would not emerge again as a military threat to David.

Third, in 2 Samuel 8:3-8, David defeats the Arameans. He defeats the king of Zobah and his Aramean reinforcements. In this battle, David captured thousands of soldiers. He also plundered large amounts of bronze—which was later used by King Solomon in the construction of the Jerusalem temple.

Then David ordered the placement of military bases within Aramean territory. The establishment of Israelite garrisons would have served to discourage the amassing of Aramean military power.

Last, in 2 Samuel 8:13-14, David defeats the Edomite armies. Following these battles, David places Israelite garrisons within Edomite territories. These garrisons are small military bases. The purpose of garrisons is to provide a constant check on Edom. Rather than waiting for Edom and the other nations to build their forces anew, the garrisons in these foreign territories would quell any rising problem before it grew. Thus, David not only defeated his enemies, but he also established a strong defensive posture in surrounding territories. This use of garrisons would serve to ensure peace during the reign of David's son, Solomon.

There are two Psalms where David addresses these battles. Psalm 60 states it was written to commemorate David's battles with the Arameans and Edomites. Psalm 60:2 speaks of the land of Israel being fractured and desperate. When considering they were surrounded by enemy nations, it makes sense the people would have been fearful. At the beginning of the psalm, David states he feels as if God has rejected Israel altogether.

In Psalm 60:10, David bemoans it appearing as if the Lord has abandoned Israel to military defeat. Years earlier, in the last major battle, both King Saul and Jonathan perished. Now that David is established as the king, he is surrounded by enemies. So David's fear makes sense. It would have indeed seemed as if God had abandoned His people. Thus, it took incredible courage and faith for David to begin his military campaigns against all the enemies in 2 Samuel 8. David responds to his fear by looking to the Lord for military victory.

It is likely Psalm 25 was also written by David to commemorate his battles in 2 Samuel 8. In Psalm 25:19-22, David speaks of the many enemies of Israel and their need for deliverance. This applies directly to this occasion because Israel indeed had many enemies at this time. Within Psalm 25, David captures some of his thoughts during these military battles. David speaks of putting his trust in the Lord for deliverance (**derealization**). In the psalm, David takes a personal inventory—asking God to forgive any hidden sins which he may have left unconfessed (Psa. 25:11). Therefore, David is making an attempt to make complete peace with God. Realizing the threat of national enemies, David wants to rid himself of any faults which may tilt the scales in the favor of his foes. Thus, David enters these military battles fully relying upon the Lord for help. In his mind, if the Lord does not help Israel, they will be defeated by their many enemies.

Dear David,

After so many years, it must have been bizarre to stand again within the gates of Gath. Many years ago you were brought there as a prisoner. Then you frequented this city during your stay in Philistine territory.

As a young man you may have never thought you would capture this great city of the Philistines. However, God has brought this great thing to pass.

Sometimes in life our later experiences can provide comfort for the past wrongs we have suffered. Your difficult history in Gath has been overwhelmed by your present victory in this city.

If I were in your position I would interpret the unfolding of these events in this way: While you were a prisoner, and while you were fleeing, God had a plan in motion to give you victory over those things.

This should give us encouragement to always "look beyond" any trial we face. All the problems this world offers are merely "temporary." All bad things pass. We can look to God who is faithful to bring us through every hardship—no matter how impossible it may seem at the time. I trust, dear friend, this thought will provide encouragement to you during your future trials.

Keep your head lifted high, dear David. Look always to the victory the Lord will bring on your behalf. Keep your heart with all diligence— leaving behind any secret sin which may hinder you in your journey.

Sincerely,
Genesis Pilgrim

Traumatic Experience 20: <u>Mercy Rejection & Ammonite and Aramean Battle</u>

Read 2 Samuel 10:1-19 & Psalms 20, 124

After a lifetime of fleeing and battles, David finally has opportunity to try a new thing: *Mercy*. For the battle-hardened warrior, it indeed takes tremendous courage to become a relational person. To survive battle, the warrior must learn to silence compassion. Combat is loud; mercy is quiet and delicate. When the warrior spends much time on the battlefield, it becomes difficult to hear the quiet things of the heart. The loss of fine relational abilities is often the first wound experienced by warriors on the battlefield. They can be regained, but it takes much effort.

After his military victories in 2 Samuel 8, King David desires to grow in his mercy and compassion. Perhaps he is sentimental at this point, remembering himself as the shepherd boy who simply cared for his sheep. Now he seeks to become the shepherd-king.

Remembering the kindness of Jonathan, David searches for one of Jonathan's family members. David finds Jonathan has a crippled son, so he takes steps to show kindness to him on behalf of his deceased father. This application of mercy was a success for David, so it encourages him to be merciful in another way . . .

In 2 Samuel 10, when David hears about the death of the Ammonite king, he chooses to send a group of officials to the Ammonite court to express sympathy. However, this attempt of mercy was not successful. The officials were abused by the Ammonite court and humiliated. Although David did right in extending kindness, he was scorned—similar to his mistreatment by Nabal in 1 Samuel 25.

When scorned by Nabal, David's mind immediately reverted back into combat mode. David's response is that of a battle-hardened leader. It is immediate and violent. David ordered his men to put on their swords (1 Sam. 25:13).

However, in this case with the Ammonite king we see David makes some progress. Rather than having an immediate, violent response to the mistreatment of his officials, David waits before commanding his army general to march out in full force against the Ammonites (2 Sam. 10:5-7). David initially responds in peace. David does not order his army to assemble until he receives a report that the Ammonites and Arameans were assembling against him.

Thus, David, a man doing his best to develop mercy and compassion, had a short fuse. In the past, this ability to respond quickly to military threats kept David safe. It gave him the advantage against all his enemies. On the battlefield, the winning army is the one which is one step faster and more proficient than the other. When weapons and equipment for the two forces are similar, speed is the one thing which allows an army to shift momentum in its favor.

So the development of a short fuse is the most decisive trait of any battlefield leader. It allows for a measured, quick response to enemy action. Often the short fuse is accompanied with PTSD, which helps the leader anticipate potential threats. The use of the short fuse allows the leader to rapidly match an anticipated action with a response that is designed to off-balance the adversary to shift momentum back into one's favor. However, when the individual is in peaceful situations, this short fuse can result in irritability, aggression, heightened startle reaction and emotional distress. In other words, the emotional response of the individual with PTSD is often incongruent with their actual surroundings.

Unlike the situation involving Nabal discussed above, in this Bible passage (2 Sam. 10:5-7), David has the sense of mind to avoid making a short fuse decision. He attempts to let the situation resolve itself, and only when the Ammonites take measures to attack David does he choose to assemble his armies against them. Thus, this is a great step for David in the development of relational mercy. During this occasion, under intense pressure to make a short fuse decision, David instead holds back and waits for the situation to develop. This is drastically different than his response to the scorn of Nabal in 1 Sam. 25:13.

To resolve this situation, David's army generals, Joab and Abishai, lead successful attacks against the Ammonites and Arameans. The Arameans later regrouped and marched to war against David. In this final battle, David was victorious. The Arameans became subject to the Israelites. In this way, David further expanded his nation's regional power. This was another step which ensured the establishment of peace enjoyed during the later reign of King Solomon.

It is likely Psalm 124 was written to commemorate this period in David's reign over Israel. In the above Bible passage, David fights the Ammonites and Arameans at the end of an extensive war campaign against the numerous enemies of Israel. Summarizing the completion of these tumultuous wars, David believes Israel would have been swept away if it were not for the Lord's divine protection (Psa. 124:1-7). Therefore it is fitting this psalm is forever remembered as one of the Psalms of Ascents. Every time the Israelites would travel to Israel for a feast, they would recite this psalm—bringing to mind all the military victories that were granted by God.

Psalm 20 was likely also written to commemorate the events of 2 Samuel 10:1-19. During this passage, David remains in Zion and he sends out Joab in command of Israel's army. Psalm 20:1-5 reads like a blessing David placed upon Joab and the fighting men as he sent them forth to fight the Ammonites. Whereas the Ammonites trusted in hiring Arameans soldiers to help them; Israel trusted in the Lord to grant them victory (2 Sam. 10:6 & Psa. 20:7). Being that he was the newly appointed king of Israel, David stresses his anointing and his identity as the "king" of the nation (Psa. 20:6, 9). Although David could not leave Zion to fight with his men, he is confident the Lord will proceed from Zion with his prayers to come to the rescue of Israel.

Dear David,

I am encouraged to see you are an outstanding leader—gathering around you many "mighty men" capable of outstanding feats. Whereas King Saul had no champion in his army to fight for him; you have many champions who serve you as mighty men and generals.

This is important. Never lose sight of this, dear David. These mighty men, capable of great deeds, will protect and fight for you in time of need. No one can stand alone.

Moreover, any army that has the ability to move forward in multiple divisions holds an advantage over an enemy with a single army. By having many leaders, your army becomes capable of moving as separate, mutually supporting units. It is encouraging to see you are applying this principle to your leadership of Israel's army.

My heart was warmed when hearing about your efforts to show mercy and kindness. It takes courage to be a merciful person. It was kind for you to care for Mephibosheth, and to also send condolences to the Ammonite royal family in the midst of their loss. Sometimes these can be great experiences—where we are met with a mutual love by the person who receives the kindness. As social creatures, it makes us feel good when we are kind to others.

But sometimes finding the right words or the right method to extend compassion can be tricky—especially if we are reaching out to a hurting family or someone with whom we have a bad history. In those cases, perhaps the best choice is to avoid it altogether. We can run into trouble in those cases, so if you are not sure, it might be good to speak to one of your candid advisers—like Nathan or Ahimelech, who can advise you on different methods to show kindness.

It is never easy to face rejection. However, it is encouraging to see you did not respond as quickly to the recent offense when the Ammonite king mistreated your officials. Rather than responding right away, in anger, you gave yourself opportunity to make a measured decision over time. Often when we feel our anger rising, it is good to step aside (if possible) to allow ourselves time to consult with a trusted adviser. This will help us to make good decisions we will not regret later.

Although this attempt at mercy was met with a bad result, let me encourage you to try again! Do not allow the evil intentions of others to quench the works of the Spirit.

Sincerely,
Genesis Pilgrim

Traumatic Experience 21: <u>Sin against Bathsheba and Uriah & Loss of Child</u>

Read 2 Samuel 11:1-12:23 & Psalms 32, 51

After a lifetime of warfare, David chooses to stay home rather than go to war. David sends his general, Joab, with the Israelite army to fight against the Ammonites. At this point, David cannot be blamed for wanting to get a break from combat. From the moment he stepped forth to fight Goliath, David faced dangers during his entire childhood and adulthood. He finally had opportunity to step away from the battlefield—to attempt to be a "normal" person. However, as we read, David made some major social missteps here.

Combat stress changes people. For many warriors, there is difficulty re-assimilating into "normal" society. It is a process. Some combat veterans need time and coaching to recapture their previous social patterns. The warrior must break free of patterns they used on the battlefield to survive.

The actions of David in this Bible passage should be viewed in light of his many combat experiences. Here is a man who for his entire adulthood never had opportunity to learn how to relate to women properly. Although he was married now, we must remember that David's "normal" childhood was deprived him due to his early success on the battlefield. So the common experience of learning how to properly relate to women was denied David.

Now, Bathsheba enters the story. David's mistreatment of this situation was the result of lack of coaching/counseling to help him to establish himself as a "normal" person. David deserved a break from war. It was okay for him to sit out the war with the Ammonites in this passage. However, the main problem was that David presumed he was like other normal citizens. Indeed, the battle-hardened warrior—to whom normal citizens owe their freedom—is not like normal citizens.

Most notable in this passage, the prophet Nathan and the priest Abiathar are absent. During this major transition in David's life—from warrior to being solo in normal society, David really needed advice. A good counselor could have presented David with options, and helped him to develop a plan to occupy himself during this transition. This plan would have helped David to keep his mind from drifting—perhaps through the use of a hobby. This is the chief problem. It was not wrong for David to stay home from the war. It was wrong, however, for others to allow him to predictably deteriorate into bad decision-making.

Nevertheless, from this battle mindset, David looks out at the city below his palace. He saw something he liked (Bathsheba), and he aggressively pursued her. David learned Bathsheba was the wife of a foreigner, Uriah the Hittite. In previous chapters, David subdued many foreign nations, so the identity of the foreigner may have consoled David in pursuing Bathsheba. After all, in David's mind, Uriah could have been little more than one of the many other foreigners he bested on previous battlefields.

After learning of Bathsheba's pregnancy, David reels on what to do next. In the passage, he sends a messenger to bring Bathsheba's husband, Uriah, to him. At this point, it appears David wants Uriah to sleep with Bathsheba so he can be duped into thinking the child is his own. When Uriah refuses to go to his house, David instead decides to have Uriah killed on the battlefield.

Loss of life is a horror common for the warrior. Having seen the deaths of many, David assigns death to Uriah. To console Joab, David tells him the sword devours all the same. This reveals David's conceptualization of battle. Death on the battlefield is mysterious. In life we often assign meaning to everything, but chaos sweeps across the battlefield. Following battles, our minds reel in their attempts to assign purpose to losses. But it is such a confusing, overwhelming process that it often cripples the mind. Thus, Uriah is fed to Chaos.

Following the death of Uriah, Joab sent a report to David. In this report, it becomes clear David had a short fuse. Joab anticipates David's anger would flare up as he hears the report of the battle losses (2 Sam. 11:20). The messenger is instructed to respond to David's anger with the news that Uriah is dead.

Often in battle, warriors develop a "short fuse" as a survival mechanism. This is a part of PTSD—as the warrior becomes capable of instantly responding to changing battle conditions. When no longer on the battlefield, this short fuse tends to stick with former warriors. The battle-scarred mind begins to interpret things through this filter. Whereas, the short fuse allowed the warrior to rapidly respond to life and death situations; the same mindset leads him to overreact to "normal" life situations.

Later, the prophet Nathan rebukes David for his mistreatment of Uriah and Bathsheba. In his discussion with Nathan, we see David has a short fuse. When hearing the story that a man took another person's lamb, David's immediate response is to pronounce a death sentence in his burning anger. This reveals David was indeed struggling with PTSD. In hearing this hypothetical scenario, David does not demonstrate the neutral judgment of a king—where he measures the offense, demands to hear witnesses and gives the accused opportunity to defend himself. Rather, David's PTSD controls his response. Not only is "death" the immediate verdict, but David also says the condemned man must pay a fine—as if to suggest further harm can be visited on a man already deceased (2 Sam. 11:5-6).

Nathan matches David's fiery anger—telling David *he* is the lamb-stealer. Nathan goes on to tell David he will be judged for his actions. In a mysterious way, David will somehow bear culpability for the death of his son. Over the course of time, David's son became ill. Perhaps as the result of David's sin, the Lord did not allow healing for the son. In this, David was brought into grief as he pleaded for the life of the child.

So, in this judgment there is equity. David caused grief to Bathsheba at the death of Uriah (2 Sam. 11:26). Perhaps, the grief for Uriah was altogether insufficient. The Lord visits grief upon David and Bathsheba to allow them to experience the full measure of grief they should have felt for the lamb, Uriah. And, just as David—the king of his people, did not value the life of the foreigner, Uriah the Hittite; so also the Lord—the Giver and Taker of life, did not value the life of David's child. So, in an equal measurement, grief was visited upon those who caused grief. God recalls the life of the son upon Himself.

Psalm 51 was written by David to commemorate these events. In this psalm, David asks God to cleanse him from his sin. David was altogether broken—feeling as if his bones themselves were crushed by his grief. In Psalm 51:11, David asks God not to remove the Holy Spirit from him. At this time in the Old Testament, the Holy Spirit was not with people permanently. This is why the Spirit of the Lord withdrew from King Saul. This is why David pleads with God not to abandon him.

The offenses of David extend beyond the brutality he showed to Uriah. David grovels before the Lord over all the offenses he did before Him (Psa. 51:3-5). David does not want to be righteous in his own sight, and viewing his sins as mere offenses against other people would have resulted in David viewing "righteousness" as an attainable human venture (Psa. 51:4). Rather, David looks to God for righteous judgment to help him to abandon false senses of self. David welcomes the harsh judgment of God so he may be truly righteous in God's sight.

Psalm 32 was likely written to commemorate how God restored David following his sin with Bathsheba and Uriah. In 2 Samuel 12:16-20, David intensely grieves for his son—who is ill as a result of his sin. This is reflected in Psalm 32:3-4, where David states his grieving was so intense it felt as if his bones were wasting away from the feverish heat of the summer. However, within this grieving, David candidly confesses his sin to God (Psa. 32:1, 5). As a result, God covers David's sin by providing forgiveness.

At the conclusion of Psalm 32, David experiences a restoration to his liturgical leadership role. God has restored David by providing forgiveness. Thus, in Psalm 32:6-11, David urges everyone to confess their own sin to receive the Lord's forgiveness. Although this incident of sin has been devastating for David, God provides a way of restoration for him. That restoration begins when David humbles himself, confessing his sin to God.

Dear David,

My advice is for you to remain occupied with tasks to keep your mind busy. Typically, combat warriors like you develop the ability to think on so many different levels. Your experiences on the battlefield have given you an acute awareness of your surroundings—where your mind becomes drawn in by certain things.

This ability can be used for your benefit. You will be forever capable of "seeing" and experiencing things that others frankly cannot. For example, you can "see" the kingdom of God around you, protecting you from danger in the midst of trouble. This is due to your traumatic experiences. However, try as hard as they might, those who have not experienced what you have may never become able of "seeing" what you "see." Thus, your trauma has purchased for you the ability to walk by faith, not by sight.

If however this ability is left unattended, it will be natural for it to be used for fallen purposes. Rather than it being intentionally used for good, it can be used in a fallen way to draw your attention to things that are not good—particularly images of a past that cannot be changed, a present that is instantly gratifying, or a future that "may" occur.

Do not allow your mind to master you. Master your own mind as you take captive every thought to obedience. When you feel things become tangled in your mind, ask a trusted counselor for help. Occupy your mind and time with good things. Do not allow yourself to be dragged along into thoughts which will lead you down a path to a false past, present or future. Do not allow yourself to be dragged into the experiences of the past. However difficult, fight those chariots when they call for you. You need not allow yourself to be transported to places where you once were.

If you ever choose to board one of these chariots, do not do it alone. Take a counselor with you. A counselor can offer perspective. Rather than you being completely drawn in by a past event, a counselor can provide a link back to the present to anchor you. This will prevent a whole bunch of potential problems that could arise from us travelling into the past alone.

   Sincerely,
   Genesis Pilgrim

Traumatic Experience 22: <u>Ammonite Battle</u>

Read 2 Samuel 11:1; 12:26-31 & Psalms 9, 51

In this Bible passage, Israel's army besieges the chief city of the Ammonites—Rabbah. After Joab cuts off the city's water supply, he sends a message to King David. Then, David arrives at the besieged city and concludes the capture. David wears the gold crown from the Ammonite king to signify the total subjugation of the defeated army.

In this passage, David plunders all the Ammonite settlements. He also takes Ammonite captives—who become labor workers for Israel. After battles with other nations, David would establish Israelite army garrisons in those foreign territories. In this passage, he does the same.

This battle and the resulting subjugation of the Ammonites took place during the Bathsheba/Uriah incident (2 Sam. 11). David met with Bathsheba after Joab and the army already marched to Rabbah (2 Sam. 11:1). Shortly after Uriah's death, the siege of Rabbah was completed. Then the confrontation between Nathan and David would have likely occurred much later—after the child of David and Bathsheba was born.

Why is this important? It is important because when David went to Rabbah, his sin against Uriah was unresolved. Although he went to Rabbah in victory, David held within him the secret sin he carried out against Uriah. David travels to the same city where Uriah was executed at his command. Thus, God does not allow David to distance himself from his sin against Uriah. Circumstances arrange themselves to bring David to the exact location where he caused the death of Uriah.

As David places the Ammonite crown upon his head, he bears within himself this secret. David continues to bear this subconscious guilt— perhaps resurfacing at different moments as he completes the Ammonite campaign with his army. David travels throughout Ammonite settlements, directing activities for captives, and returns to his palace. Later, his son with Bathsheba is born. David still carries within himself his hidden sin. Then, perhaps thinking he finally escaped God's judgment, Nathan arrives.

Earlier when David sent Joab to Rabbah, he used his time *destructively*. David made bad decisions with his treatment of Bathsheba and Uriah. Now that the Ammonite war in Rabbah is complete, David is once again within his palace and at peace. However, now this time will be used *constructively*.

As I stated earlier, a warrior like David needs a coach/counselor to help him to properly re-assimilate into "normal" society. The difference between these two situations of peace is that in the first case, David was not attended by a coach/counselor. Thus, David made terrible decisions with Bathsheba. Now, however, in the second case, David is attended by his counselor, Nathan.

Of what benefit is a counselor? Psalm 51 is the answer. Without a counselor, the battle-hardened David was left to make bad decisions. However, with the counselor Nathan to put him on the right path, David here is able to use his time of peace for deep self-reflection. Psalm 51 is the result. Nathan, as the counselor, was the catalyst which allowed David to grieve, grovel and grow. This is why a warrior needs help when re-entering "normal" society. Abandoning the former warrior to himself will be *disastrous*, but providing timely counsel can be *constructive*.

Psalm 9 was likely written to commemorate David's experiences in this Bible passage. Earlier, a coalition of Ammonites and Arameans fled from Israel in battle (2 Samuel 10:14-19 & Psa. 9:3). Now, in 2 Samuel 12:26-31, David gains a decisive victory over the Ammonites—uprooting their cities (2 Sam. 12:31 & Psa. 9:6). David goes to the gates of the city of Rabbah to complete the siege, then brings back the Ammonite crown to the gates of Jerusalem. This is reflected in Psalm 9:13-14 as David goes to the gates of death, then returns victoriously to the gates of Zion. By removing the crown of the Ammonite king, David causes the past splendor of Ammon to perish from memory (Psa. 9:6).

Dear David,

When we make mistakes, sometimes we think we can get away. But God always gives us opportunities to come to terms with the wrongs we have done. God blesses us with opportunities where our sins are brought to the front of our minds.

I can imagine what it would have been like for you to walk through the gates of Rabbah—to the same place where Uriah died. My goal is not to judge you, but to offer you counsel—to give you encouragement.

Be assured, no matter what we have done wrong, God offers to us a path to restoration. It might not be easy, and we may have to endure great punishment as a result of our wrongdoing, but be confident in this fact: God never takes pleasure in the death of the wicked, but desires for all people to come to repentance. As long as we have life, we have opportunity to change.

We need not abandon ourselves to our past mistakes. If we did this, we would all perish under the weight of past burdens. We can choose, however, to learn from our mistakes. We can choose to look at what we have done wrong—making the decision to change our behavior as God gives us the ability to do so.

In this present thing you have done, my advice is for you to let it all out. Discuss with your counselor exactly what you did wrong—what you regret and would desire to change. There is a path which leads out of the deep trench in which you find yourself. Do not abandon yourself in your present condition. Allow the Lord to counsel and guide you out of that dark place where you can admit to your faults and live the rest of your allotted days in faithfulness.

Life is indeed precious. Although life has been lost, there is nothing to be gained by allowing yourself to be abandoned. Allow your remaining life to be a source of vitality to others. Dedicate your life to re-building what was broken in your past.

> *Sincerely,*
> *Genesis Pilgrim*

113

Traumatic Experience 23: Eluding Capture from Absalom

Read 2 Samuel 15:10-37; 16:5-14 & Psalms 3, 22, 27, 55, 101, 143

David's sin with Bathsheba and Uriah foreshadowed future problems within David's family. The incident with Absalom follows the prediction that strife would not depart from David's household (2 Sam. 12:10-12). Both incidents occurred as a result of David's failure to exercise good judgment.

In 2 Samuel 13, David's son, Amnon, raped his step-sister, Tamar. One of David's nephews even helped Amnon to plot this wickedness (2 Sam. 13:3). Sadly, when David heard about this he did nothing. The Bible says David was angry, but he took no action to get justice for Tamar (2 Sam. 13:21).

Why did David fail to take action? In the earlier chapter he was quick to pronounce the death sentence in a hypothetical situation involving a man stealing another man's lamb. Now, however, David is emotionally crippled. He merely has anger when receiving the news that his own daughter was raped. Why?

At the least we see David lacks the skill to deal with this situation because it is a family issue. In other cases David shows he is capable of rendering judgment to "normal" citizens. However, when this matter occurs within his own household, he becomes angered then does nothing. It might be best to view this as a part of David's PTSD social impairment. He cares enough to be angry, but he lacks the delicate social skills to navigate his way through the situation. Therefore, he avoids it altogether.

As is often the case, when people do not receive justice they take matters into their own hands (Ecc. 8:11). Realizing that his sister would not receive justice, Absalom (another son of David) murders Amnon. Upon learning of Amnon's death, David mourns for many days (2 Sam. 13:36-38). Similar to his lack of action following Tamar's rape, David here has a complete lack of action. Rather than pursuing justice against Absalom, King

David seems to be satisfied with unofficially exiling Absalom (2 Sam. 13:38-39).

Perhaps at this point, David avoids pursuing Absalom due to his own history of being pursued by King Saul. Although David wants reconciliation with Absalom, he is reluctant to leave the palace to go to him (2 Sam. 14:1). Nevertheless, Joab, David's army general, plots with Absalom to have him brought back into the king's good graces.

In all this, the inaction of David is viewed as a vulnerability. Absalom muses on the inaction of the emotionally crippled king who failed to give his sister Tamar justice. Although appreciated at the time, Absalom now despises David for failing to attempt to punish him for murdering Amnon. In Absalom's mind, the decisiveness and prowess of David is now gone. He is no longer fit to be king because he cannot even govern his own household. Thus the prophecy of 2 Sam. 12:10-12 is fulfilled. Absalom decides to declare himself king (2 Sam. 15:10).

Upon hearing of Absalom's treason, David decides to flee from the palace. For David this experience would have been traumatic. As a young man, David fled for years from King Saul. Now, as an older man, David flees from Absalom. Both Saul and Absalom were improper "kings," being appointed at the will of the people rather than the initiative of the Lord (1 Sam. 8:6 & 2 Sam. 15:10). Both Saul and Absalom were permitted to live only at the mercy of David. Saul survived multiple occasions where the Lord delivered him to David. Absalom was permitted to remain in exile rather than facing the king's justice. Thus as David sets out from the palace, his mind would have been brought to remember that similar experience fleeing from Saul.

David was convinced he would be captured and put to death if he remained in the city (2 Sam. 15:14). David escapes danger by fleeing into the wilderness with his household and some of his trusted officials. As was his common practice, David brings Abiathar the priest with him. Additionally, David sets out with the ark. Upon completing sacrifices, David instructs some of the priests to take the ark back into the city. This is significant because it shows David desired the blessing of the Lord during this troublesome time.

Furthermore, David looks to the Lord as his ally. He prays for God to frustrate the military tactics of Absalom (2 Sam. 15:31-34). In earlier battles, David viewed the Lord God as a warrior who fought on his behalf. Likewise, during this time of crisis, David looks to the Lord to deliver him from trouble. Just as He was faithful in the past, so here the Lord shows his faithfulness to protect David.

As David travels further from the city, a man named *Shimei* ridicules him (2 Sam. 16:5-8). Earlier in 2 Samuel 13:3, a son of *Shimeah*—David's brother, helped Amnon develop the plot to rape Tamar. Interestingly, the both of these men's names mean "*fame*." Thus, we can see a theme concerning how David was negatively affected by "fame." Although people many people desire to be famous—renown in the sight of people ultimately serves to be a source of grief. Fame in David's life makes his family the target of plots. Fame also puts him high atop a pedestal—where he later receives public ridicule.

Rather than fighting the cursing from Shimei, David receives it humbly. He prevents his soldiers from putting Shimei to death (2 Sam. 18:9-12). David explains he wants God to stand up for him rather than avenging himself. Just as David refused to raise a hand against Saul, the Benjamite, so also he refuses to raise a hand against Shimei, the Benjamite. In the former case, God delivered him from Saul—ultimately proving all his words as empty threats. Likewise, David trusts God will rebuke Shimei.

Psalm 3 commemorates David fleeing from Absalom. In this psalm, David shows his vulnerability. He is concerned with the many people who are threatening him. However, we see David chooses to wait patiently for the Lord's deliverance.

David is honest in his prayers—giving God his unfiltered thoughts. In Psalm 3:7, David asks God to strike the jaws of his enemies, breaking their teeth. The Psalms teach us prayer should contain our unfiltered thoughts. If we think it, we should say it to God. Then, through our honesty with God, He is able to work with us to help us break free from extreme emotions—such as anger.

David is able to rest in the midst of danger. In Psalm 3:5-6, David declares he finds complete security even though he is surrounded by his enemies. The ability to dissociate from one's surroundings is a symptom of PTSD—as the individual develops the ability to survive through extreme situations. David's spirituality was a result of his PTSD. When in danger, David could spiritually "see" God's protection as a mighty fortress, stronghold and shield around him. Thus, David learned to walk by faith, not by physical sight. Here in this case, David's ability to dissociate allowed him to experience complete peace even though he was surrounded by enemies.

Other psalms contain details that could be describing this situation—including Psalm 101, 55, 22, 143 and 27. Each psalm contains different snapshots of David's thoughts as he survived through this situation.

Psalm 101 may commemorate the thoughts of David during the exile of Absalom following the murder of Amnon (2 Sam. 13:38-14:1). In this psalm, David states he is doing his best to live a blameless life by keeping sinners in his household away from him (Psa. 101:2-4). He states he will not allow these sinning relatives to enter his presence (Psa. 101:6-7). This is how David chose to relate to Absalom after failing to render justice after Amnon's rape of his half-sister Tamar.

Whereas David completely failed to provide justice to Tamar; he now moves in the other extreme—declaring that even those who are suspected of secret sins will be expelled from his family (Psa. 101:4-7). This demonstrates the complete social impairment of David—which is a common symptom of PTSD. David is socially awkward. He fails to judge rape, yet is incredibly harsh on lesser issues—like secret sins he imagines within other's hearts. David is doing his best to navigate an incredibly difficult family crisis, but clearly he needs the advice of a skilled counselor.

In Psalm 55, David is consumed with negativity as he is dragged into this hardship. He describes his feelings of distress within the city before he flees. This could capture the depth of emotion he felt before fleeing and in the first several days. In this situation he experiences the worst betrayals as some of his closest allies turn against him (Psa. 55:13-14).

David's physical reactions through his PTSD are extreme. He mentions fear which causes his entire body to tremble (Psa. 55:5). His PTSD also causes his heart to feel anguish—likely a sinking, racing feeling (Psa.55:4). These physical symptoms are persistent, with David noting his state of distress continues throughout each day (Psa. 55:17).

David's mind works against him by building up negative images that keep him stuck in this rock-bottom state. He imagines he can hear the words of his enemies as they plot against him (Psa. 55:3). In Psalm 55:6-8, David expresses the desire to fly away. When a person does not have an outlet for these extreme emotions and physical reactions, it is no wonder why people turn to substance abuse—including drugs and alcohol. In all these things, David is describing his own PTSD symptoms which were caused by his years of combat and now comprise the mental framework through which he interprets all his experiences.

In Psalm 22, David expounds on his feelings of fear. His mind races through visions of his isolation with enemies surrounding him. In Psalm 22:1-2, David becomes anxious in his prayers, being impatient in his distress—wanting God to immediately speed him to deliverance. He imagines even God has forsaken him. Racing, exaggerated thoughts are a symptom of PTSD. However difficult to navigate at the time, these thoughts provide a means for deeper spirituality.

Often David's mind races through extreme negative images, then they give way to positive images that are equally extreme. This allows the person with PTSD to use their mind to "see" things others cannot. Although PTSD brings the person through deep "lows," the spiritual "highs" can be just as extreme. Thus, at the core of spirituality is the ability to focus one's mind on the unseen. PTSD grants the individual the ability to have dramatic, heartfelt responses which correspond with their thoughts.

Indeed, surviving through difficult times might make people better equipped to accept the gospel (Matt. 25:34-36). A person who has spent time surviving through sickness, imprisonment, hunger and physical stressors may more readily gain the ability to "see" with spiritual eyes rather than physical eyes. The more one walks through hardship, the more their heart is prepared to walk by faith not by sight. David might have been terrified as his mind raced through the negative images, but this same attribute was what made it possible for him to continually "see" God around him as a great fortress of protection (Psa. 2:12; 5:11; 7:1; 8:2; 9:9; 11:1; 14:6; 16:1; 17:7; 18:2, 30-31, 46; 19:14; 25:20; 27:1, 5; 28:1, 8; 31:1-4, 19-20; 34:8, 22; 36:7; 37:39-40; 40:2; 52:7; 55:8; 57:1; 59:1, 9, 16-17; 61:2-4; 62:2, 6-8; 64:10; 95:1; 141:8; 142:4-5; 144:1-2). This is a result of PTSD derealization.

Moreover, PTSD contributes to messianic prophecy through depersonalization. Physical disorders such as PTSD, indeed granted the prophets a means through which God provided visions—where the prophet would become detached from himself momentarily to describe a future situation experienced by or near the Lord Jesus (Psa. 2:6-9; 8:2-6; 16:10-11; 41:9; 68:18; 109:8; 110:1-7). Suffice it to say that although PTSD is a disabling physical condition, it can provide an incredible benefit in the development of personal spirituality.

Furthermore, PTSD in leaders, such as David, has played a vital role in the development of Christian spirituality throughout Biblical history. Faith itself has been built upon the aftermath of traumatic experiences. Trauma is a plowed field; faith is the life that springs forth. The plow of trauma is vital to prepare the soil for the growth of faith. Without trauma there is no basis for faith. This is perhaps why the Lord Jesus commands his followers to focus their ministries upon those who have experienced trauma (Matt. 25:31-46). Those who suffer trauma have within their hearts fields plowed and prepared for the growth of faith.

In Psalm 143, David is in the wilderness being pursued by an unnamed enemy—conflating David's past fleeing from Saul and his present fleeing from Absalom. Here David waits for guidance from the Lord (Psa. 143:8). This could mean Psalm 143 was written to commemorate the evenings following the offering of sacrifices in the wilderness as David waited for the Lord's guidance to come to him in the morning (2 Sam.

15:24-28). In 2 Samuel 17:15-16, David received an answer to this prayer when his spy sent him a helpful report detailing Absalom's military plans.

In Psalm 143:3, David explains his emotional distress causes his spirit to grow faint. This could be a reference to the racing heart beat and other physical effects which often accompany PTSD panic attacks. It makes sense David would be experiencing these symptoms because he believed he was in danger of being killed (Psa. 143:4-7).

In Psalm 27, David steps away from the negativity and focuses his mind on positive things. Although David acknowledges he is still being pursued by an army, he chooses instead to dwell on the Lord's protection. He states he will seek the Lord, desiring to dwell in His house. He patiently waits for the Lord and puts his confidence in His coming deliverance. This shows the transition that occurs in David's mind as he uses his powerful PTSD abilities for good within himself. He chooses to use the strong visualization of the mind to build up positive images to provide a framework for him to move forward in faith.

Dear David,

It can be difficult dealing with tough social situations—especially when family members commit serious crimes against one another. Problems become worse when the head of the household is also the king—making you the highest official to render justice in the nation. So what would be the best way to respond in the situations you face?

It might be good for you to appoint an official who can render judgment in such situations. This would allow you to remove yourself from being the judge over serious crimes that have been committed by a family member, while still ensuring crimes are punished. It is not good to avoid rendering judgment altogether because people will want to take justice into their own hands.

After messing up, you may feel tempted to give up. It may seem an enticing option to withdraw altogether from social settings—passively drifting through each day. However, let me encourage you to remain actively engaged within your life.

One of the most important things for men is to remain emotionally available to their loved ones. Just as God did not exile you for your sin, it is also not good for you to exile others for sins. If you were to exile every sinner, the entire nation would be emptied. So if you do not have the strength or ability to render judgment in cases of crimes, then consider appointing a good judge to do so on your behalf.

Sincerely,
Genesis Pilgrim

Traumatic Experience 24: <u>Death of Absalom</u>

Read 2 Samuel 18:1-5 & 18:33-19:7; 1 Kings 1:5-27 & Psalms 21, 41

In this Bible passage we see the conclusion of the Absalom rebellion. The report from the spy gave David's military a great advantage over Absalom's army. Armed with the knowledge of Absalom's plan, David had confidence. David's generals urged him to remain away from the battlefield for his own safety. David granted their request. In return David told his forces to be gentle with Absalom. Although David was sure he would win the battle, he still wanted to save his son's life. Then David's army left to prepare an ambush for Absalom.

Unaware that David received advanced information of his plans, Absalom also was confident of victory. In 2 Samuel 18:9, it says Absalom rode a mule into battle. Typically mules or donkeys, being less agile than horses, were ridden in times of peace—not onto a battlefield. Thus, Absalom was likely so sure of victory he thought he was only going there to give his victory speech.

However, the Lord favored David. On the battlefield David's army defeated Absalom's military. As he fled, Absalom became tangled in the branches of a tree. Joab, David's general, killed Absalom.

Upon receiving the battle messenger, David immediately asked about Absalom. At all costs David desired for his son to be saved. David was devastated when told Absalom was slain. He declared it would have been better for him to die than for his son.

The grief of David is irrational. In his mind he overlooks all the faults of Absalom—the murder of Amnon and also his treason in declaring himself king and rallying the entire country to kill David. The king who is quick to issue judgment upon other citizens is completely incapable of rendering any judgment on his own family members—even in the case of murder, rape and treason. Why?

This is likely due to the social impairment that is a common symptom of combat PTSD. Navigating family relationships takes a great deal of finesse. Often the trauma of the battlefield can cause the loss of this delicate ability. Thus, when viewing the intimate relationships David had with his family members we see he demonstrates this type of social awkwardness.

This is further seen in the fact that after he left his parents' household, his brothers and parents are almost completely absent from his life—with the exception when he was visited by his family at the Moab stronghold (1 Sam. 22:3). In his reflections upon his relationship with his parents, David states he felt completely rejected by them from childhood (1 Sam. 16:11 & Psa. 22:10; 27:10; 69:8). This means the PTSD social impairment of David affected all his relationships and would have been clearly recognizable.

Thus, in the case of Absalom, David is found to be socially awkward, lacking the ability to properly conceptualize the actions of others and to respond properly. Joab is candid in pointing out David's social impairment. Joab tells David he hates those he should love, and loves those he should hate. Essentially, David is so socially awkward his behavior inadvertently gaslights his entire army—resulting in them feeling humiliated and attempting to feign grief for simply winning a battle.

At this point, Joab is fed up with David, similar to how Absalom was fed up with him. Earlier, after David failed to properly deal with Amnon's rape of Tamar, Absalom decided to rebel. Now, having viewed David's failure to properly judge Absalom's treason, Joab tells David he will completely remove the army from his kingship if he does not change his behavior.

Overall, David had many problems resulting from his combat PTSD. His social impairment was so severe it crippled him emotionally. He was incapable of properly judging situations where his family was involved. This symptom of David's PTSD had disastrous effects for the entire kingdom—resulting in national crisis and the loss of thousands in Absalom's rebellion.

Later, the social impairment of David again nearly causes a national crisis. In 1 Kings 1:5-27, another son of David, Adonijah, declares himself to be David's successor. In light of David's social impairment, this should be viewed as the result of David's inability to properly relate to individuals in his own family. As he aged, David should have developed a plan to turn over leadership. Instead, he does not think to do so until there is another national crisis brewing as a result of his inaction.

Therefore, the social impairment of David is not simply the result of normal oversights. Rather it is the result of a PTSD symptom which defines his persisting behavior. David simply did not fit in with people. He was an exceptional warrior, capable of anticipating the actions of adversaries on the battlefield. But, while reigning from the safety of his throne he was emotionally crippled and nearly blind in reading subtle relationship cues from others. Those closest to David saw this clearly. As a result, they gently walked him toward the right social actions. This is seen clearly in 1 Kings 1:11-20 when the prophet, Nathan, and Bathsheba discuss how to gently move David toward making a good decision.

Whereas Joab attempts to "fix" David by telling him to change his behavior; the prophet, Nathan, attempts to gently guide David to the right social answer (2 Sam. 19:7 & 1 Kings 1:13-14). When assisting a person with PTSD, the approach of Nathan is best. A person with PTSD may be impaired in their ability to navigate social issues. Gently assisting them in making the right decision is the best approach. Attempting to "fix" a person using a direct approach would be as cruel as ridiculing a person in a wheel chair for sitting too long. In these cases, David likely wanted to make the right social decisions, but his PTSD condition resulted in him feeling incapable. He needed the help of people who were skilled in social interaction.

Psalm 21 may have been written to commemorate the anointing of Solomon to succeed David as king. Solomon was granted the desire of his heart when God declared he would give him wisdom (Psa. 21:2 & 1 Kings 3:5-14). Solomon was also granted long life and blessing that far exceeded other kings (Psa. 21:4, 6). Unlike David, who was anointed then lived for many years before being crowned as king; Solomon was greeted at first with a crown of gold at his anointing (Psa. 21:3). The peaceful reign of

Solomon was made possible by the many military victories of David (Psa. 21:5).

Shortly after David appointed Solomon king, he warned him of certain troublemakers who would cause harm to his kingdom (1 Kings 2:5-9). These potential troublemakers included Joab and Shimei. Additionally, Solomon would have to deal with opposition from his brother, Adonijah, who still desired to gain the throne for himself. Psalm 21:8-12 refers to Solomon's upcoming conflicts with these individuals. Although Solomon would be spared from participation in full-scale war, he would still need to confront those who sought to do evil within his kingdom.

It is likely Psalm 41 was written to commemorate the sickness experienced by David in 1 Kings 1:1. In Psalm 41:4, David asks the Lord for healing—both physical and spiritual. Meanwhile, David suspects there are many plotting against him during his time of illness (Psa. 41:5-8).

Psalm 41:9 mentions a betrayer who has lifted up his heel against David. Perhaps the betrayer identified by David here is Adonijah—one of the sons of David who advantageously gathered officials and declared himself king during this period (1 Kings 1:5). It could also be that the betrayer of Psalm 41:9 is Abiathar the priest, or Joab (1 Kings 1:7). Indeed, Abiathar the priest may be the best option for the betrayer because David would have prayed and worshipped with him many times during their travels after the incident at Nob.

Furthermore, this psalm contains messianic prophecy describing the betrayal of the Lord Jesus. Whereas the "betrayer" in the life of David was either Abiathar, Adonijah or Joab; the "betrayer" of the Messiah was Judas. The psalm concludes with David peering out into eternity with the Lord. He is confident he will remain in the presence of the Lord forever (Psa. 41:12-13).

Dear David,

I am saddened to hear of the loss of your son.

Giving ourselves opportunity to grieve is very important. Attending a funeral will help your mind to gradually come to grips with the loss. Regardless of the circumstances of the loss, all families should grieve the fallen—telling stories of the good times.

In the past you did not have opportunity to grieve for the priests of Nob and this was not good. But you did have opportunity to grieve for Saul, Jonathan and Abner—this was proper. In this case, please ensure you are properly grieving for Absalom to allow your heart to be comforted, my dear David.

Try to put out of your mind the offense of Joab. War is a stressful thing for all people involved. It is natural for sorrow to arise and for tempers to flare.

As a warrior and a commander of armies, it is not likely you will ever respond well to direct rebuke. Perhaps as you age in your throne you can keep a gentle adviser, like Nathan, near you. He could help you process information carefully while reducing the pressure you might feel to make quick decisions. Being gently guided and advised in your decision-making is much better than feeling as if you are being confronted and insulted by blunt people.

It might be a good decision to create a buffer within your court to receive the harsh reports for you so you can interact with the information through your adviser. This would prevent you from feeling as if you are being thrown into chaos and forced to instantly react—as if you are on a battlefield while you are in your palace. The key is to protect your mind from situations in which you will feel stressed.

Sincerely,
Genesis Pilgrim

Traumatic Experience 25: <u>Last Philistine Battle</u>

Read 2 Samuel 21:15-17 & Psalms 18, 38, 69

Following the defeat of Absalom, David returns to Jerusalem. David remains wary of his general, Joab, after he threatened David in 2 Sam. 19:7. When another traitor arises, named Sheba, David issues orders to his other army generals rather than Joab (2 Sam. 20:4-6). This shows David lost his confidence in Joab. This is seen further in 2 Samuel 20:7 where all the soldiers from Joab's command are assigned to another general. In response, Joab kills a general, named Amasa, and takes back command of his troops (2 Sam. 20:8-13). Joab ensures the death of the traitor, Sheba, then he returns to David in Jerusalem.

Similar to his earlier inactions, David neglects to punish Joab for his murder of the army general, Amasa. David's social impairment prevents him from rendering judgment upon Joab. Yet in a bizarre fashion, King David unflinchingly commands the deaths of seven descendants of Saul in 2 Samuel 21. So, whereas David would not punish a murderer in his own court; David chose to put seven men to death to atone for unseen offenses that were revealed in prayer to have resulted in a three year famine.

This example demonstrates the dramatic social impairment of David—where he unequally and improperly applied the law to citizens (Deu. 24:16). Apparently, being close to David granted immunity for crimes—regardless of severity—including rape, murder and treason. However, he would grant death to citizens for offenses they themselves did not commit. Although death was more readily administered in the ancient world, David nevertheless needed to have a skilled person appointed within his court to ensure the proper application of justice. This would have allowed David to effectively govern while accounting for his PTSD social impairment disability.

In 2 Samuel 21:15-17, David participates in the last military battle of his career. In this battle, he becomes physically exhausted and nearly dies. But one of David's generals, Abishai, steps into the gap to rescue

129

David from a giant enemy, named Ishbi-Benob. Thus, the military exploits of David began as they ended—with empty threats of an enemy and a slain giant. The first giant's name was Goliath—and rightly so because *splendor* was offered to any with the mettle to defeat him. This last giant's name was Ishbi-Benob, meaning simply that he *dwelled in Nob*.

The mention of Nob (high place) in the giant's name may have done certain things within the mind of David. Perhaps David was brought to remember the town of Nob he visited as he fled as a young man from King Saul. Or perhaps, David's mind was brought to remember the many priests who perished at the cruelty of Saul in that city. Alas, it may be the "exhaustion" of David was brought on at the realization he visited a similar cruelty upon the seven sons of Saul.

In Nob, people died for the supposed sin of another; now David realizes he committed a similar act in ordering the deaths of sons for the sin of their father. He remembers the gentle rebuking action of Rizpah, who cared for the bodies of the dead, and may have thought back to his own innocence in desiring to offer some relief to Nob after the deed was reported to him (2 Sam. 21:10-12).

Indeed, at this time, and in the context of 2 Samuel 21, it might be that the *name* of Ishbi-Benob was the trigger for a wave of intense emotions stretching back to David's youth. He realizes he has allowed himself to mirror the actions of the king he once fled. The shepherd-king David is gripped as his mind races away from the battlefield, while his body remains immersed in the midst of imminent danger. David's general, Abishai, steps in to rescue David, and in a great act of concern, boldly commands David to forever remain away from all future battlefields.

There are several psalms which may commemorate David's close brush with death in this final battle. These could include Psalms 38, 69 and 18.

In Psalm 38:7-10, David discusses his racing heartbeat and a feeling of doom as his strength fails on the battlefield. This fits with the events of 2 Samuel 21:15-17. Here in Psalm 38:2, David interprets his failing strength as the result of God's judgment upon him. David feels overwhelming guilt, but we are left to wonder *why* he feels guilty (Psa. 38:4). As discussed above, it is likely David is overwhelmed by his guilt for mistreating the descendants of Saul. Psalm 38 concludes with David crying out for the Lord's deliverance (Psa. 38:22). God answers this prayer as he sends Abishai to save David (2 Sam. 21:17).

In Psalm 69:1-15, David discusses a sinking feeling—as if he is drowning in the midst of an overwhelming enemy army (Psa. 69:4). This is likely a crippling PTSD panic attack that surfaces while David is on the battlefield of 2 Samuel 21:15-17. His mind races from the circumstances of the battlefield—where he is outnumbered, to visions of his past betrayals within the city. Thus, the racing thoughts of the panic attack could be the "exhaustion" experienced by David in 2 Samuel 21:15. On the battlefield, David needs clarity of mind to focus on the enemy before him. But a panic attack causes his heart to race and his mind to scatter over past experiences—reacting strongly to multiple situations simultaneously.

In Psalm 69:6-12, we see the PTSD social impairment of David. He explains he feels as if he is the cause of shame experienced by others. He feels a vast separation from his own parents and family. Last, he describes the numerous insults he perceives others have for him and his religious beliefs. Of course, there were likely not many who would dare insult King David directly. Thus this statement of "insults" is more telling of David's mental state in "imagining" the insults of others. Overall, when considering the experiences of David as a whole, this passage in Psalm 69:6-12 further supports the fact that David was socially impaired as a result of his PTSD.

Some of the details in Psalm 18 apply to different situations because David was delivered from all battlefields throughout his life. Although situations appeared hopeless at many times, God was faithful to deliver David from them all (Psa. 18:1-2).

However in Psalm 18:4-6, David is likely commemorating his near death experience on this specific battlefield. In the case of 2 Samuel 21:15-17, God rescues David through the action of the general, Abishai. In this way, Abishai proceeds forth as a messenger from the Lord. The arrows and weapons of Abishai are imbued with divine power as he rescues God's anointed king.

Within the context of this near death experience, David experiences derealization. Even though he was nearly killed on the battlefield by Ishbi-Benob, David rejoices in his own physical strength—stating he has the agility of a deer and the strength to bend a bow of bronze (Psa. 18:32-34). In this way, the PTSD of David enables him to maintain extreme courage and confidence—even when he was physically exhausted to the point of death.

The detachment from physical reality afforded through derealization can be a decisive factor on the battlefield. The warrior who thinks himself strong may become capable of gaining a second wind of effort, thus gaining a decisive advantage over their enemy. Even when brought to his culminating point, a spiritual warrior can re-vitalize himself through his "connection" with the supernatural (2 Cor. 12:10).

The Angel of the Lord imagery of Psalm 18 provides a link between the life stories of Moses and David. Whereas Moses met with the Lord face to face, and followed Him in the pillar of cloud and fire; David was also sustained by the Angel of the Lord in all his battles.

Moses began in the court of Pharaoh; David began in the court of Saul.

Both men were driven into the wilderness—Moses to Midian; David to exile throughout the wildernesses of Israel and the Philistine territories.

Both return from exile—Moses back to lead his people out of Egypt; David back to be crowned king of Judah, then Israel.

National peace was also purchased through the efforts of both men—Moses leading Israel to the borders of the Promised Land; David successfully fighting all his nation's enemies to purchase the national peace enjoyed during Solomon's reign.

Throughout their lives, the Angel of the Lord was instrumental in many national events—including events of judgment, such as Meribah and the threshing floor of Araunah the Jebusite. The Angel of the Lord also moved at various times to fight for Israel.

Psalm 18 commemorates the national reliance upon the Lord Himself for governance, thereby linking the reign of David to Moses. Neither Moses nor David desired honor or privilege. Moses was declared to be the most humble man; David was the shepherd-king. Throughout the "reigns" of both men, they pointed to the Lord Himself as the ultimate ruler of the people. Thus, it is fitting that the king who glorified the Lord in his reign will also share in the joy of the Lord's eternal reign.

Dear David,

Your recent close call on the battlefield serves as a great reminder of how we rely on other people. At one point or another, we will all need another to carry us. It is humbling to be carried upon a stretcher, but this provides good medicine for our hearts. Just as we were born and were totally dependent on our parents, so throughout our lives we learn we never lose reliance upon God and those He sends forth to help us.

It is good you have surrounded yourself with "mighty men" and champions to help you in your role as the judge and king of Israel. God was faithful to call you, just as He called Moses and the Judges. Just as He was faithful to watch over those leaders, so He will continue to watch over you.

Panic attacks can be frightening. They cause our hearts to race and a whole bunch of other effects. When you feel your body is starting to spiral out of control, it is good if you have the ability to step away from whatever is causing the stress.

It is a good decision to remain away from battlefields from now on. After all, you have many "mighty men" who can fight with valor and skill on your behalf. On battlefields you place yourself in a situation where you cannot take a break. There is no reason to hurt yourself in this way. After the many years your body has served you, it is good for you to look after your body. Be mindful of your heart and stay away from these stressful situations.

Sincerely,
Genesis Pilgrim

Traumatic Experience 26: The Census Plague

Read 2 Samuel 24:1-17 & Psalm 18

Following Abishai's victory over the giant Ishbi-Benob, the remaining three Philistine giants were defeated (2 Sam. 21:18-22). Then in 2 Samuel 22, David reflects on God's protection during all his battles. This song is also shown in Psalm 18.

In 2 Samuel 23, there is a time jump where the final words of David are discussed. It is fitting that following the final battle of David we see he ended his life in faithfulness to the Lord. His last words capture how David's reliance on the Lord remained his defining characteristic all the way to the moment of death.

Moreover, the account is completed by also honoring the valiant men who served under David's command. David's life was protected by both the Lord and his valiant soldiers—thus, 2 Samuel 23 contains a final tribute to both. The successes of David also belong to the Lord and his valiant soldiers.

This brings us to the last traumatic experience of King David: his numbering of Israel and the resulting plague. In Scripture, taking a census was not inherently evil. Earlier God commanded Moses to take a census of Israel (Numbers 1:1-4). But David's motive and method were both conflicted—and thus unacceptable.

Why did David number the fighting men of Israel? Remarkably, the Bible says both the Lord Himself, and also Satan prompted David to order the census (2 Sam. 24:1 & 1 Chr. 21:1). How is this possible?

Perhaps the purpose for David wanting to conduct the census was at first right and noble. He may have been moved at first out of a good purpose to number Israel at the end of his reign to provide a roster for the king who would succeed him. However, as things often do, the original good purpose—being directed by the Lord, may have been corrupted by Satan as he caused pride to grow within David. As his pride increased,

135

David may have allowed himself to think himself a "superior" king—being the cause of all good things that led to Israel's national prowess.

A fitting royal parallel, which also provoked immediate judgment from God, is found in Daniel 4:28-33. Nebuchadnezzar, king of Babylon, was the person upon whom God built the entire Babylonian kingdom. This was good and according to God's purpose (Dan. 4:19-22). However, the fallen mind of Nebuchadnezzar twisted that good purpose as he was led astray by Satan. Nebuchadnezzar, looks out at his kingdom, and thinks of himself in the highest esteem, thereby provoking immediate judgment from the Lord. Thus it is best to apply this same type of inner confliction to David. He originally started with good purpose, but he became corrupted as his mind was drawn away from it.

The *method* of David's census was also corrupted. Whereas the census of Moses required each tribe to participate in the overwhelming task numbering citizens; the census of David placed this incredible burden upon the army officials themselves (Num. 1:4 & 2 Sam. 24:2). In Moses' census there was no requirement placed upon census officials necessitating separation from their families (2 Sam. 24:8). However, in David's census, the army officials spent nearly 10 months away from their families—travelling to every area of Israel's territory.

The theme here is that David sinned by viewing all his people, and even his trusted army officials, as mere numbers. Not only did the army officials bear the burden of fighting for the nation, but now they were sent on a pointless fool's errand for almost an entire year. Moreover, the army officials were not provided a justification for the census itself, with David saying the purpose was only for his own knowledge (2 Sam. 24:2). Frankly, this is not the purpose of army officials. They deserved respect and instead these mighty men were slighted by their king.

This information helps us understand the punishment choices presented to David by Gad the prophet. The Lord decided David would be punished—and all three punishments had severe implications for Israel as a whole. The choices were: (1) three years of famine, (2) three months of military defeat, or (3) three days of plague from the Angel of the Lord. David selects the third option.

So, how can the three choices be reconciled? Why were these three options presented? The three choices are not arbitrary—each choice is connected to a natural outcome that "could" result from the census.

The second option of military defeat is relatively easy to explain within the context. The army officials were already slighted by David's method of census. Although the army soldiers were many, the census errand would have incited many of the army officers against David. Thus, the Lord prevents the potential coup that would have formed—thereby saving Israel from a potential civil war and the opportunistic arrival of foreign armies.

In my other books I examine how the forces of darkness affect the earth. Although it is my personal thought, I present theories which detail how Satan attempts to move the earth in a fallen direction, while the Holy Spirit restrains and counters to maintain the earth (Psa. 104:30). Therefore, my opinion is that the three years of famine was "going to" happen. But for God to prevent it, the Angel of the Lord needed to do certain things in the region to check the advancements of the forces of evil. So, in the presentation of the three choices to David, to prevent the first choice (three years of famine), God had to do specific things in the environment—directly resulting in the third choice (three years plague) occurring as a side effect of the prevention action taken by the Lord.

This is significant because it maintains what we know of the Lord—He is always good. The three options were not arbitrary. Rather, by presenting the choices to David He shares with him a sample of the decisions which He resolves constantly to maintain the earth until the day when everything can be restored. The Lord could have allowed the three years of famine to occur by doing nothing to check the forces of darkness. But in order for the Lord to check the forces of famine, he needed to either: (1) misdirect the forces of darkness from the environment onto the surrounding regions/people bringing on war, or (2) confront the forces of darkness directly in three days—causing collateral damage within the territory of Israel. This is why I am convinced those specific choices were presented to David.

Nevertheless, David thinks himself totally responsible for the harm which befalls Israel (2 Sam. 24:17). He pleads with God to stop the plague. Then David offers sacrifices to the Lord in the location where his eyes were opened to the spiritual conflict that was occurring (2 Sam. 24:18-25).

This event was significant for David. The ordering of the census is the last great act of David. As the narrative moves forward into 1 Kings 1, we see David is crippled—physically and mentally. He no longer makes big decisions—perhaps due to his reluctance at his great misstep in ordering the census.

David does not even take measures to appoint a successor to his throne. This means the census was a major turning point for David. Previously David was diligent in storing up vast provisions for the future king to use in the construction of the temple. But now in 1 Kings 1, David idly occupies the throne, taking no action to continue his efforts to set up his successor for success. It takes the prompting of Nathan, the prophet, for David to re-engage with his royal responsibilities (1 Kings 1:11-14).

Therefore, the census incident was significant for David. He dared not risk any further action to inspire God's judgment. Even in the case of selecting his own successor, David waits for the Lord to send His prophet to provide specific guidance. The census experience ushered David to the realization he could no longer trust his own judgment.

Dear David,

Feeling the guilt of having made a mistake, you may feel inclined to withdraw. Let me encourage you to see through your tasks to completion. You spent many years fighting the battles of the Lord—building up the peace and prosperity that will be enjoyed by future generations. You gathered materials to build the Lord's temple—even though you are not to build it yourself.

Realize your life is not the end of something. Rather your life is the beginning of a spiritual journey that will be travelled by people who walk in your footsteps—being energized by your writing, inspired by your faith, and encouraged by the deliverances of the Lord continually realized through your life. You will serve as inspiration to the many generations of God's people who will live after you.

Be encouraged, friend. Finish your good work. Consult with Nathan, the prophet, and appoint the successor to your throne.

Then rest in peace, my dear David, until the Day when you arise to receive your allotted inheritance.

In Christ,
Genesis Pilgrim

Section 2: David's PTSD Symptoms & the Symptom Psalms

(Psalm 5, 6, 8, 11-14, 16, 19, 28, 36, 37, 39, 53, 62, 64, 68, 109, 110, 140, 141)

Symptom Psalms are psalms in which David simply vents to the Lord. Unlike "Experience Psalms," Symptom Psalms do not contain clear details which allow us to narrow them down to a specific event in David's life. However, Symptom Psalms are useful in showing us the thought patterns of David—including how he viewed God, himself and others.

In this section of my book we will examine the Symptom Psalms of David by providing notes from these psalms to demonstrate David met the diagnostic criteria for PTSD. Below the various criteria and symptoms for PTSD have been abbreviated and summarized for simplicity. *For complete study on the topic of PTSD, consult the DSM-5 (Diagnostic and Statistical Manual of Mental Disorders, 5th Ed., American Psychiatric Association, American Psychiatric Publishing, 2013).*

Disclaimer: This book is not intended to diagnose readers with PTSD. If you, or anyone you know, is struggling with trauma, seek the advice of a licensed counselor. A licensed counselor can properly evaluate psychological disorders and provide a treatment plan, including cognitive processing therapy (CPT), to help you on the road to recovery.

How David Fit PTSD Criteria

Below the various PTSD criteria are listed, along with brief paragraphs describing the relevant experiences of David. When reading these paragraphs, it should become clear David had PTSD connected to his past traumatic experiences.

Direct Exposure to Trauma: Death, Threatened Death, Serious Injury, Violence

David had many experiences where he was exposed to direct trauma. The earliest experiences mentioned by the Bible occurred when David killed the lion and the bear (1 Sam. 17:34-36). As a young boy he defeated Goliath in single combat (1 Sam. 17:33). Moving forward through his life, David was then subjected to repeated threats on many battlefields (1 Sam. 18:13). David was also the subject of plots by King Saul to take his life. David narrowly escaped capture by Saul on multiple occasions (1 Sam. 23:7-12, 25-28).

Witnessing Trauma: Death, Threatened Death, Serious Injury, Violence

During the many battles of David he would have witnessed trauma occurring all around him. These events would have included loss of life and injury on many battlefields.

Learning Relative/Close Friend Experienced Trauma: Death, Threatened Death, Serious Injury, Violence

David had several traumatic experiences when hearing of the deaths of those he knew. The first occurred when he learned King Saul executed the citizens of Nob (1 Sam. 22:22). On this occasion, David declared himself responsible for all the deaths—even though he did not commit the acts himself.

Later, the deaths of Jonathan and Saul were significant for David (2 Sam. 1:11-27). During his reign as king, David set in motion events that also led to the murder of two generals—Abner and Amasa. Although David did not play a direct part in their murder, it is likely David struggled with a sense of personal involvement. This can be supported by his later statement in carefully articulating blame on the murderer himself (1 Kings 2:5).

Perhaps the most significant emotional response was witnessed in David's mourning following the report of Absalom's death. It is likely within the death of Absalom David experienced flashbacks of previous losses for which he considered himself ultimately culpable. Although David did not directly cause the deaths of the citizens of Nob or Absalom, he viewed himself as the root cause for the losses.

Indirect Exposure in Course of Professional Duties (First Responders, Medics, Etc.)

David was instructed to mutilate Philistine corpses to collect foreskins for King Saul (1 Sam. 18:15-27). As previously discussed, I am convinced this act was commanded as an intentionally humiliating act of public mockery. King Saul commanded this to intentionally damage the young David's mind and morality (1 Sam. 18:20-25). David was so loyal that he carried out the order as a part of his professional duties to King Saul. However, it is likely this experience later caused guilt, shame and embarrassment for David.

Symptoms Not Due to Medication, Substance Abuse or Other Illness

In 1 Kings 1:1, it states David struggled to stay warm as he aged. This is likely a common thing experienced by most people as they are in their senior years.

In the Psalms, it appears David did have some heart disorder—which would account for him stating his heart is in anguish and grows hot. However, this heart condition may be a symptom of PTSD itself. It is common for PTSD sufferers to experience panic attacks. Racing heart beats and a sinking feeling in the chest can occur as a result of PTSD.

For these reasons, it is likely David did not have another illness other than PTSD.

Moreover, there is nothing to indicate David was involved in substance abuse or the use of a medication which would have caused side-effects similar to PTSD symptoms.

Symptoms Persist After Trauma Long-Term

In order for symptoms to be considered "PTSD" they must persist long-term in the individual. Nearly all humans have traumatic experiences. Whereas some people are able to heal from trauma; in others the symptoms of the trauma continue to affect the individual long-term.

In the Psalms of David, it is clear his many traumatic experiences continued to affect him for the duration of his life.

David's PTSD Symptoms

Below, PTSD symptoms are listed in alphabetic order. For each symptom, I provide information from David's life and writing in the "Symptom Psalms" to demonstrate how David exhibited each respective PTSD symptom.

At the end of each symptom discussion, I provide page references where the respective symptom is also referenced throughout my book. When reading below, it should become clear David exhibited PTSD symptoms connected to his many traumatic experiences. Indeed, David's PTSD symptoms are clearly seen throughout his writing in the Psalms.

(If you are interested in reading more about a specific PTSD symptom exhibited by David throughout his life, please consult Index #2 for a full, condensed reference of each PTSD symptom and the page numbers where they are mentioned in this book.)

Avoidance of Trauma-Related Thoughts/Feelings

Perhaps the most prominent example of David's avoidance of trauma-related thoughts/feelings occurs following a family crisis. The Experience Psalm 101 may commemorate the thoughts of David during the exile of Absalom following the murder of Amnon (2 Sam. 13:38-14:1). In this psalm, David states he is doing his best to live a blameless life by keeping sinners in his household away from him (Psa. 101:2-4). He states he will not allow these sinning relatives to enter his presence (Psa. 101:6-7). This is how David chose to relate to Absalom in the aftermath of Tamar's rape and Amnon's murder.

Whereas David completely failed to provide justice to Tamar; he now moves in the other extreme—declaring that even those who are suspected of secret sins will be expelled from his family (Psa. 101:4-7). Rather than attempting to navigate this complex social situation, David's PTSD compels him to avoid it altogether.

(For further study, more notes on David's "Avoidance of Trauma-Related Thoughts/Feelings" can be found on pages 115, 118.)

Avoidance of Trauma-Related External Reminders

In Psalm 6:8, David desires to have all potentially evil people removed from his presence. This demonstrates David's avoidance of one of his chief trauma reminders: people. During many of David's traumatic experiences, other people betrayed him. Here in Psalm 6, David intends to avoid all people who could "potentially" betray him.

(For further study, more notes on David's "Avoidance of Trauma-Related External Reminders" can be found on page 45.)

Decreased Interest in Activities

We are left to assume the primary activity enjoyed by David was writing and leading/teaching congregations in spiritual principles. (We will explore this topic of the **Seeing Psalms** further in the last section of this book.) Unfortunately, the Bible does not provide information on other hobbies enjoyed by David.

If David's spirituality was in fact his favorite activity, then we know he experienced difficulties in this area. At times David felt detached from God. David felt as if God had abandoned him or was punishing him at different stages in his life (Psa. 13:1-4; 39:10-13). This means David experienced decreased ability to pursue his favorite activities as a result of his PTSD symptoms.

(For further study, more notes on David's "Decreased Interest in Activities" can be found on pages 91, 115, 124-125, 138.)

Depersonalization

The PTSD symptom "depersonalization" is a type of dissociation which occurs when the individual experiences feeling detached from oneself. This results in the individual feeling as if they are in a dream or as if they are an outside observer.

In various Psalms of David his mind turns to descriptions of events fulfilled during the life of the Messiah, the Lord Jesus Christ. So, it could be possible these messianic prophecies are revealed to David as the Holy Spirit communicates through this PTSD symptom of David. In other words, the PTSD of David provides a natural, explainable channel through which God can communicate prophecy.

Thus, the messianic prophecies of David demonstrate he experienced "depersonalization." Some of these messianic prophecies of David can be found in these Symptom Psalm passages: Psa. 8:2-6; 16:10-11; 68:18; 109:8; 110:1-7.

Furthermore, David often experiences events from within other people—likely in a dream-like or vision state. In some of his social impairment, David actually interacts within the mind of other people—reflecting on their motives and thoughts (Psa. 5:9-10; 12:1-4; 28:3-4; 36:1-4; 62:3-4; 141:8-10). These examples of depersonalization likely lend to David's social impairment as he interacts with his presumed image of people, rather than interacting with them as they choose to present themselves.

(For further study, more notes on David's "Depersonalization" can be found on pages x-xii, 31, 57-58, 83, 101, 120, 126, 131, 164-169, 172-173, 175, 178-182, 195-196, 199-200.)

Derealization

The PTSD symptom "derealization" is a type of dissociation which occurs when the individual experiences feeling as if their surroundings are not real, at times choosing to hold to an unseen reality. This results in viewing one's surroundings in ways they would not be interpreted by unaffected individuals. Thus, an individual experiencing derealization may view reality in a manner which would be described as "distorted" or "unreality" from the unaffected perspective.

The most pronounced way in which David experienced "derealization" was in his view of God. Similar to how Ezekiel later saw God's glory as a giant supernatural structure over Jerusalem, David consistently discusses God as the supernatural refuge/stronghold/fortress/shield which overshadows and surrounds him in the midst of all his troubles. David's derealization can be found in these Symptom Psalm passages: Psa. 5:11-12; 6:10; 11:1; 12:5-7; 14:2, 5-7; 16:1, 5-8; 19:1-4; 36:5-7; 37:2-40; 39:10-13; 62:2, 6-8, 12; 68:1, 5-6, 9-10, 22-23.

These Psalm passages show David experienced derealization— "seeing" God as providing unseen support to the poor, needy and faithful persons, while simultaneously punishing wicked people in unseen ways. Similar to Ezekiel's later vision, David also views the Lord as residing above the structure surrounding David (Psa. 14:2). From atop this supernatural structure, the Lord looks down to direct his blessing and punishment upon humanity. In Psalm 19:1-4, David states the heavens speak supernaturally to instruct the hearts of humans. Perhaps this is accomplished through the unseen fortress of the Lord which resides above and around David in the sky.

Within David's derealization, he also "sees" God interacting with the congregation of the faithful. In Psalm 68:2-35, David describes God as moving out to protect His people as at the Exodus. God provides salvation to those doomed to die (Psa. 68:20). He also empowers the faithful (Psa. 68:35). In Psalm 36:5-7, David "sees" God's presence extending into the skies as great wings of shelter protecting the faithful. In Psalm 37:2-40,

David discusses how he sees God meting out blessing and punishment among humanity.

To the unaffected person, this is a mere imagination or mere poetry; however David walked in faith, not by sight. On battlefields David found courage as his spiritual mind was able to "see" God's presence above and surrounding him. Thus, David's PTSD "derealization" is the natural means through which God communicated comfort to him and strengthened his faith. David's derealization provides a remarkably means through which David interacts directly with God.

Moreover, David's derealization also provides a means of self-reflection as he views God's corrective action molding his behavior. In Psalm 39:10-13, David feels as if the Lord is gazing upon him in judgment of his sin. In Psalm 39:10-13, David thinks God is against him and deaf to his prayers. David feels as if God hit him with His hand and has abandoned him to death. In Psalm 16, David explains he views the Lord as being at his right hand—providing instruction to his heart at night.

(For further study, more notes on David's "Derealization" can be found on pages x-xii, 6, 10, 26, 27, 31, 35, 45, 47, 51, 57-58, 62, 69-71, 77, 82-83, 87, 96-97, 101, 108, 116-121, 125-126, 130-133, 135, 138, 164-169, 172-173, 183-187, 189-197, 199-202.)

Difficulty Concentrating

Within the Psalms we can conclude David would have experienced an extreme deficit in his ability to concentrate in social settings. Whenever David found himself within cities, surrounded by people, his mind began suspecting people of plotting against him (Psa. 5:9-10; 12:1-4; 28:3-4; 36:1-4; 37:12-14, 32; 62:3-4; 141:8-10). It is likely David would not have been able to maintain focused conversations in these settings as his mind raced to identify potential threats in his surroundings.

(For further study, more notes on David's "Difficulty Concentrating" can be found on pages 75, 91.)

Difficulty Experiencing Positive Affect

As seen throughout the Psalms, David's relationship with God was the central part of his being (Psa. 27:4). However, David on occasion thought God may have abandoned him. In Psalm 13:1-3, David feels as if he is altogether abandoned by God—which he believes will ultimately cause his own death. A similar passage is found in Psalm 28:1-3. These passages show at David's core he had difficulty experiencing positive affect. This thought shook David to his core and robbed him of experiencing joy at those times.

(For further study, more notes on David's "Difficulty Experiencing Positive Affect" can be found on page 26.)

Difficulty Sleeping

In Psalm 6:6-7, David has difficulty sleeping as a result of emotional distress. Rather than falling asleep, David explains he remains awake and cries throughout the evening.

(For further study, more notes on David's "Difficulty Sleeping" can be found on page 26.)

Emotional Distress

The PTSD symptom "emotional distress" occurs when an individual is exposed to a traumatic reminder. A "triggering" reminder of a traumatic event could be *conscious* (with the individual recognizing it immediately), or it could be *subconscious* (where the individual feels emotionally distressed incongruent with their surroundings without knowing why). Today, counselors can assist those with PTSD in the identification of "triggers" and their causes through treatments like "cognitive processing therapy" (CPT).

In Psalm 5:1-2, David experiences emotional distress (lamenting, crying). The traumatic reminder is found in Psalm 5:9-10—where David imagines people in a social setting plotting against him. This would remind him of traumatic occasions in his life, such as the plotting of the Saul's officials before he was compelled to flee.

In Psalm 6:2-7, David experiences emotional anguish which results in weeping and groaning.

In Psalm 13:2, David feels as if he is having to wrestle his own heart, day after day.

In Psalm 39:2-3, David mentions changes in his heart during his emotional anguish. It is likely this could be a panic attack—which may cause the heart to sink, race or feel different.

(For further study, more notes on David's "Emotional Distress" can be found on pages 26, 46, 47, 62, 77, 83, 92, 100, 107-108, 118, 120, 124, 130-131.)

Exaggerated Blame of Self or Others for Causing the Trauma

Early in David's life, he declares in 1 Samuel 22:22 that he feels responsible for the deaths of all the people at Nob. Then, most notably, during all the pursuits of Saul, David refuses to harm Saul. In this way, David wrongly presumes a type of divine impunity upon Saul (1 Sam. 24:6; 26:9). Thus, David thinks himself unworthy of justice as he constantly feels as if he must move to remain outside of Saul's reach (1 Sam. 27:1). In this way, David seemingly presumes a type of guilt upon himself for being pursued by Saul. David believes he must subject himself to perpetual suffering for all of Saul's life—perhaps for somehow failing Saul or even for failing the people of Nob (1 Sam. 26:19).

(For further study, more notes on David's "Exaggerated Blame of Self or Others" can be found on pages 5, 39-41, 81, 123, 129, 138.)

Feeling Isolated

In Psalm 12:1-4, David declares there are no faithful or loyal people. This shows David had a social impairment which led him to complete feelings of isolation when triggered.

In Psalm 13:1-4, David feels completely isolated from God. Yet in this desperate feeling, David still wrestles in prayer to have God "take him back." This shows David felt as if he had absolutely nowhere else to turn—further illustrating his intense feelings of isolation.

In Psalm 39:10-13, David feels isolated from God—imagining God is deaf to his prayers. David feels as if God hit him and has doomed him to die.

In Psalm 109:2-5, David discusses his feelings of isolation from his many presumed enemies.

(For further study, more notes on David "Feeling Isolated" can be found on pages 5, 11, 58, 62, 96, 108, 119, 171.)

Flashbacks

In Psalm 13:2, David states he experiences sorrow in his heart day after day as he reflects on how his enemies have supplanted him.

Elements of flashbacks may also be seen in extreme emotional responses of David which are incongruent with his surroundings. In many of the psalms where David is interacting with thoughts of those around him plotting against him, David's intense emotions do not match his actual surroundings.

Rather than allowing for someone to commit a crime, then addressing the crime, David jumps to major conclusions. He sees people whispering in the city—assuming they are whispering about him. Then he assumes they are whispering about killing him. Overall, this is a pattern which indicates David may be experiencing flashbacks of his earlier betrayals. His mind wrongly conflates those intense emotions based on past events with his present surroundings.

(For further study, more notes on David's "Flashbacks" can be found on pages 3, 45-46, 58, 61, 69-70, 82, 116, 120, 130-131.)

Heightened Startle Reaction

David exhibits a heightened startle reaction. When insulted by Nabal, David's reaction was immediate and violent (1 Sam. 25:21-22). In 2 Samuel 1:14-16, David's anger flared up against a man who presumably performed an act of mercy. In 2 Samuel 11:20, Joab expected for David's anger to flare up upon receiving a certain battle report.

Overall, David had a habit of responding in a manner incongruent with the situation presented. At times he did not make measured, appropriate judgments. Therefore, we should conclude David would have had a "heightened startle reaction" as a symptom of his PTSD.

(For further study, more notes on David's "Heightened Startle Reaction" can be found on pages 58, 83, 100, 106-107.)

Hypervigilance

In Psalm 140:2-8, David exhibits hypervigilance. He suspects those around him have set traps for him. This would have resulted in David guarding himself as he searched for the hidden agenda of people he suspected of plotting against him.

Moreover, in 2 Samuel 17:8, it is acknowledged that David—as an experienced fighter—would anticipate the actions of enemies. Then he would position himself so that he could maintain an advantage. This demonstrates David was highly vigilant on the battlefield as well as within social settings.

(For further study, more notes on David's "Hypervigilance" can be found on page 57.)

Inability to Recall Key Features of the Trauma

A psychologist would be able to determine if David experienced "inability to recall features of trauma" through a psychological evaluation. Typically, "cognitive processing therapy" (CPT) could be used to determine what an individual remembers about a traumatic event. When considering the other symptoms of David's PTSD, it is likely he would exhibit this symptom as well.

His social impairment seems to indicate David struggled to correctly judge the motives and actions of others. This may be due to David's inability to properly label past betrayals he suffered and to interact with each based on its own circumstances. Thus, David interacted with all social situations as if they could be betrayals. This means that David's mind likely would have had problems recalling the key features of many of his previous traumatic events.

(For further study, more notes on David's "Inability to Recall Key Features" can be found on pages 6, 20, 45, 69-70, 82, 120.)

154

Irritability or Aggression

In Psalm 109:5-20, David expresses aggression toward his "presumed" enemies. Although his enemies have not yet committed a crime against him, David asks God to judge them to the maximum. This shows David's PTSD mind would make assumptions, then jump to conclusions based on those assumptions.

In PTSD the mind makes assumptions in an effort to protect the individual from a perceived risk which somehow reminds the brain of a previous traumatic event. Once triggered, the PTSD mind jumps to conclusions to help prepare the individual for an imminent attack. This is why David's mind often jumped to conclusions when he found himself in social situations.

(For further study, more notes on David's "Irritability or Aggression" can be found on pages 11, 51, 57, 67, 83, 99-100, 106-107, 117, 119, 129.)

Negative Affect

In Psalm 13:1-3, David feels as if he is altogether abandoned by God—which he believes will ultimately cause his own death. A similar passage is found in Psalm 28:1-3.

In Psalm 16:2, David states he has nothing good in his life apart from God.

In Psalm 39:4-13, David takes a pessimistic perspective on life—dwelling on the immanence of his own death and the deaths of others.

(For further study, more notes on David's "Negative Affect" can be found on pages 10, 92, 106, 108, 118.)

Nightmares

In Psalm 6:6-7, David reports difficulty sleeping as a result of emotional distress. Rather than falling asleep, David remains awake and cries throughout the evening. It is possible this was due to experiencing nightmares—as intense, unresolved emotions came to the surface of his mind during REM sleep. At times he may have remained awake to avoid nightmares.

(For further study, more notes on David's "Nightmares" can be found on page 26.)

Overly Negative Assumptions about Oneself or the World

In Psalm 12:1-4, David declares there are no faithful or loyal people. This shows David had a social impairment which led him to complete feelings of isolation when triggered.

In Psalm 14:3, David declares there is no one who is righteous. He thinks of all people as being corrupt.

In Psalm 39:1-2, David is self-condemning, refusing to allow himself to speak because he is convinced he will sin (see also Psa. 39:9).

In Psalm 62:9, David states that people amount to nothing. He declares that social status means nothing.

In Psalm 141:3-4, David assumes if God allows him to speak he will commit sin. Therefore David views himself so negatively that he does not even permit himself to speak.

(For further study, more notes on David's "Overly Negative Assumptions" can be found on pages 25, 56-58, 97, 108, 138.)

Physical Reactivity

The PTSD symptom "physical reactivity" occurs when an individual is exposed to a traumatic reminder and experiences physical symptoms. A "triggering" reminder of a traumatic event could be *conscious* (with the individual recognizing it immediately), or it could be *subconscious* (where the individual feels a physical symptom incongruent with their surroundings without knowing why).

In Psalm 6:2-7, David experiences physical symptoms which accompany his emotional distress. These physical symptoms include weakness and body aches in Psalm 6:2. He also experiences restlessness in Psalm 6:6-7, where paradoxically he needs to rest his eyes, but his emotional distress does not permit him to fall asleep.

In Psalm 39:2-3, David mentions changes in his heart during his emotional anguish. It is likely this could be a panic attack—which may cause the heart to sink, race or feel different. Heart disorders, like atrial fibrillation, can develop with PTSD. Therefore, David's frequent references to his heart/spirit may indicate David developed a heart disorder as a result of his PTSD.

(For further study, more notes on David's "Physical Reactivity" can be found on pages 26, 46-47, 58, 61, 92, 107-108, 118-120, 130-131.)

Risky or Destructive Behavior

David was a fierce fighter—which demonstrates he was risky. Perhaps this PTSD symptom took root very early in David's life after he killed the lion and the bear (1 Sam. 17:34-36). As a young boy he was risky in volunteering to face Goliath in single combat. King Saul interpreted David's action here as self-destructive, being sure the novice David would be defeated by the veteran Goliath (1 Sam. 17:33).

David maintained this trait as a part of his PTSD for the rest of his life. During the Absalom rebellion, David was referred to as a wild bear robbed of her cubs—the most remarkably destructive, brutish creature in the wild (2 Sam. 17:8).

(For further study, more notes on David's "Risky or Destructive Behavior" can be found on pages 11, 99.)

Social Impairment

The PTSD symptom "social impairment" occurs when the individual experiences problems navigating common social settings. This could affect the person's ability to properly maintain relationship and occupational responsibilities.

In Psalm 5:9-10, David imagines he cannot trust anything that is spoken to him. This would present a great impairment to David as king. He consistently struggled with his distrust of people in social settings, such as cities and within his court. When considering the many traumas experienced by David in cities, it is no wonder why his mind would have developed the PTSD perception which immediately associated groups of people with danger.

For example, as a young man, David was betrayed within the city of Saul and forced to flee. David was later captured by the Philistines and brought before King Achish—where he narrowly escaped death which would have most likely been similar to the fate of the judge Samson. Thus, from his early trauma, David persisted in social impairment where he consistently associated social settings with danger—ever suspecting people of plotting against him.

In Psalm 12:1-4, David declares there are no faithful or loyal people. This shows David had a social impairment which led him to complete feelings of isolation when triggered.

In Psalm 28:3-4, David doubts and suspects people of plotting against him. This is severe—with David believing he will die if God does not help him (Psa. 28:1). David asks God to judge these people for their "suspected," unproven crimes (Psa. 28:3-4). This demonstrates David would often leap to great conclusions in his assumptions about people— suspecting them of hidden sin and desiring judgment upon them even before they could carry out any act of sin.

In Psalm 36:1-4, David suspects the inner motives of people— imagining they are plotting to do evil even as they lay down to sleep. Psalm 37:12-14 is similar. Psalm 37:32 is extreme—where David imagines these people plotting murder.

In Psalm 62:3-4, David suspects people of plotting against him. He even suspects those who speak blessings to him.

In Psalm 141:8-10, David believes he will die as a result of the plots against him. His only way of deliverance is to ask God for help. This shows the social impairment of David was often so severe that he felt in danger of losing his life.

(For further study, more notes on David's "Social Impairment" can be found on pages 5, 9-11, 14, 21, 25, 57-58, 70, 77, 82, 105, 115-116, 118-119, 123-126, 129, 131, 136, 163, 171.)

Unwanted Upsetting Memories

Perhaps the most significant indication of David's unwanted, upsetting memories can be found within his extreme "social impairment." David was originally a shepherd boy—at home in the wilderness alone with his flock (1 Sam. 16:11).

Early in David's life he began to associate cities with danger. He was betrayed by Saul and his officials within the "city" and subsequently compelled to flee (1 Sam. 19:11-18). Later he was captured by the Philistines and brought before King Achish in the "city" of Gath (1 Sam. 21:10-15). David was nearly captured by Saul within the "city" of Keilah (1 Sam. 23:7-12). As David's life continues he experiences many instances of danger within cities. It is no wonder why so many of David's psalms—penned from within the "city" walls of Jerusalem—focus greatly upon his perception of social plots.

This is a result of David's PTSD. His mind interpreted mass groups of people as dangerous in an effort to protect him from falling into the same traps he experienced earlier in his life.

(For further study, more notes on David's "Unwanted Upsetting Memories" can be found on pages 14, 40.)

Conclusion on the Symptom Psalms
Who is the "Fool" of David? (Psalm 14:3 & 53:1)

Throughout the Symptom Psalms above we see the unfiltered mind of David. The Symptom Psalms do not refer to specific experiences in David's life. Rather they are general reflections on his thoughts which he likely had at many points in his life.

In closing, I would like to discuss the "fool" of David because this is a passage which can be misunderstood if used improperly as a mere derision to people without faith. The "fool" of David is found in two psalms—Psalm 14 and Psalm 53. Interestingly, these psalms mirror one another—so it is likely David wanted to put a "double" emphasis on this to ensure that readers understand.

So, who is the "fool?"

In Psalm 14:3 & 53:1, David states the fool is any person who denies God in his heart. When reading further, and understanding David's view of God, we are able to understand why he views denial of God as foolish. For David, God was the refuge/fortress/stronghold/deliverer which enabled him to survive the trauma of many battlefields. Likewise, David encourages people to believe in God as their refuge—which they will also need in time of trouble.

In Psalm 14:5-6 & 53:5, David provides an analysis of the faithless people he has witnessed upon battlefields. David declares these people were overwhelmed with dread. But for those who believe, God is "felt" within their midst—providing them with an inexhaustible source of supernatural strength.

Thus, for David, the "fool" is any person who rejects the thought of relying on God for protection. As it has always been throughout myriad generations of humanity, trauma will occur. David declares any person is better off if they are able to rely upon both the natural and supernatural in these times of great need.

David had many desperate, hopeless situations he faced where he would have been utterly hopeless without his belief in God. Therefore, for

David, a person who unduly dismisses the possibility of God—which could be of incredible benefit to them in trouble—is indeed foolish.

When the day of trouble approaches, we need as many allies as we can find. It is indeed foolish to dismiss the greatest Ally on principle, abandoning ourselves to the trenches alone. No matter what, we will face trauma in this life. When all others abandon us, our faith in God can sustain us. Thus, the time-tested warrior, David, counsels his readers to never rule out God. He is the most important Ally we have on the battlefields of life. His combat trauma has taught him to rely upon the "unseen" God—drawing from an unlimited source of power in times of distress.

The goal of the above section of my book was to provide basic information on how David potentially fit PTSD criteria. For complete information on PTSD, or to research this topic further, consult the DSM-5 *(Diagnostic and Statistical Manual of Mental Disorders, 5th Ed., American Psychiatric Association, American Psychiatric Publishing, 2013)*.

Disclaimer: This book is not intended to diagnose readers with PTSD. If you, or anyone you know, is struggling with trauma, seek the advice of a licensed counselor. A licensed counselor can properly evaluate psychological disorders and provide a treatment plan, including cognitive processing therapy (CPT), to help you on the road to recovery.

Section 3: David's PTSD Perception of Reality & the Seeing Psalms

(Psalm 15, 24, 29, 65, 70, 72, 95, 103, 122, 131, 133, 145)

Seeing Psalms Written During Periods of Isolation

Seeing Psalms, where David's writing focuses simply on teaching people to "see" God, may also be associated with this period in David's life before and after the transportation of the ark to Jerusalem. The only PTSD symptoms found throughout these psalms are depersonalization and derealization. During this stage, David was focused on serving as a liturgical leader of Israel, so these Seeing Psalms are focused on the exclusive goal of teaching people; not his typical candid, emotional venting found in his other psalms. As such, depersonalization and derealization were intended to be carried forth as spiritual distinctive of Biblical faith. In this section of my book we will examine the Seeing Psalms of David—providing insights on the teachings of each psalm.

It is likely David wrote many of these Seeing Psalms during periods of withdrawal from people. This would explain why the Seeing Psalms do not contain many of the social impairment elements found elsewhere in other psalms. If David was somewhat isolated from people as he penned these Seeing Psalms, this means his mind might have been able to achieve some freedom from the thoughts of plots and betrayals he often imagined.

Some of these periods of isolation may include: the period after Uzzah's death, David's seclusion after the rape of Tamar and murder of Amnon, and the period of time following the death of Absalom. During these periods, David experienced withdrawals—where it is likely he secluded himself and viewed his primary contribution to Israel being spiritual in nature. Thus, the Seeing Psalms discussed in this section were likely written during these periods, or in the period of time right before David attempted to first move the ark to Jerusalem.

Seeing Psalms Transform Faith through Derealization and Depersonalization

God does not cause the bad experiences of David. But, God uses them for the spiritual benefit of David and later believers (Rom. 8:28). So why did David experience so many bad things?

David had traumatic experiences so he could be used by the Holy Spirit to develop Biblical concepts of faith. Indeed, traumatic experiences are the cause for faith. PTSD as a psychological disorder is the mechanism which processes the trauma. And at the end, in David's case, all that remains is a powerful perception of God based on his PTSD symptoms. Therefore, Biblical faith is the result of the PTSD symptoms of David.

The concepts of "believing" in the unseen, walking by faith not by sight, and the ability to "see" the supernatural kingdom of God are all based on the PTSD symptom of derealization. David filters out all of the negative aspects of PTSD through his suffering and his psalms leave future generations with a conception of faith as supernatural vision of an unseen kingdom as a fortress/stronghold/refuge. Biblical faith is centered upon the influential faith of David. He taught us to "see" the unseen through his PTSD.

Moreover, the concept of prophecy was transformed by David's PTSD. Prior to David, messianic prophecies focused on impersonal traits, such as simply stating the Messiah would be a prophet like Moses (Deu. 18:15). However, David's type of messianic prophecy is born from the PTSD symptom depersonalization. Therefore, David's prophecies do not simply state traits of the Messiah. Rather, David's prophecies describe events from within or near the Messiah as they later occur in history.

This is why David's messianic prophecies are often unclear in whom they are describing. For example, as David may be referring to himself or Solomon, he shifts without clear transitions into descriptions of the future Messiah. Therefore, David's ability to separate from himself as a part of his PTSD depersonalization is the primary contributor to the development of messianic prophecy. This is such a remarkable advancement in theology. Future prophets throughout the Bible will adopt this depersonalization method of messianic prophecy due to David's remarkable influence.

To summarize, Biblical faith exists in its present form as a result of David's PTSD. In essence, Bible-believers willingly take upon themselves a form of PTSD derealization to allow them to walk by faith, not by sight (**derealization**). In his life, David took the hardships of trauma upon himself, filtered out all the "bad" stuff, and left future believers with the positive benefits of derealization and depersonalization. As such, Biblical faith is an effective, proven tool to equip and help people to process trauma.

David lived a traumatic life to give us the ability to "see" God's kingdom. Later, the Lord Jesus died in order to make this kingdom a physical reality.

The Seeing Psalms incorporate concepts which are a result of David's PTSD symptoms of depersonalization and derealization. Depersonalization can be seen in David's messianic prophecies in these Seeing Psalm passages: Psa. 24:7-10; 29:10-11; 72:5-11, 17; 103:19-22; 145:1-2. Derealization can be seen in these Seeing Psalm passages: Psa. 15:1; 29:3-10; 65:1-13; 70:1, 5; 95:2-7; 103:6-22; 122:7-8; 131:3; 133:3; 145:3-20.

Overall, the presence of PTSD symptoms in Seeing Psalms show God intended to use the PTSD symptoms of David to teach the faithful to incorporate these practices into their own spirituality—even in cases where others did not have PTSD themselves. Below we will discuss each of the Seeing Psalms of David . . .

The Seeing Psalms

Psalm 15

In Psalm 15, David focuses on teaching people those behaviors which are acceptable to the Lord. In other words, Psalm 15 could be considered the "Law of David." Here within these simple verses, he exhorts the people to be righteous through speaking truth, doing right in their relationships with neighbors, refusing bribes, lending money without interest and separating themselves from vile people. By doing so, David explains a person can become spiritually welcome within the house of the Lord (Psa. 15:1).

Psalm 24

David experiences depersonalization in Psalm 24:5-10 as he witnesses the arrival of God within the city gates. In this vision of the future, David sees God arriving as the Savior who vindicates his people (Psa. 24:5). Here God has physical, human features. Similar to how the Lord spoke to Moses face to face, here David also mentions the face of the Lord (Exo. 33:11 & Psa. 24:6). Similar to how the Lord walked within the Garden of Eden, the Lord Himself walks in through the gates of the city (Gen. 3:8; John 12:12-15 & Psa. 24:7).

This depersonalization is powerful as it allows David to "see" the glory which would arrive in Jerusalem with the future Messiah. When David reflects on how he once entered the gates of Jerusalem as the conquering king, his mind is shifted to a depersonalization where he experiences the arrival of the King of heaven—the Messiah (2 Sam. 5:6-7 & John 12:12-15).

David experiences derealization in Psalm 24:1-2 as he sees the world around him as a product of God's supernatural creation. This may not be readily apparent to others who deny God, however David clearly views the existence of people and the earth itself as an extension of God's goodness.

Psalm 29

David experiences derealization in Psalm 29:3-9 as he discusses the changes wrought in the earth as a result of the voice of the Lord. When David views nature, he sees it as being actively shaped by the creative power of God's voice, similar to how God's voice directed creation itself (Gen. 1). This is sufficient to show us David saw God's supernatural works as influencing everything around him.

Last, in Psalm 29:10-11, David experiences depersonalization as he views God as the supernatural King, sitting upon His heavenly throne atop the seas of the earth. From this heavenly throne, the Lord looks upon the actions of humans below Him. Throughout his life, David's experiences of sitting upon thrones before people allowed him to "see" the way in which the Lord Himself presides over all of creation (Isa. 6:1 & John 12:41). No matter where David travelled in the past, he is confident he never moved outside of the supernatural gaze of the Lord.

Psalm 65

David experiences derealization in Psalm 65:1-13 as he thinks of God dwelling within His house in Jerusalem. From this location, God answers prayer, forgives sin and chooses people to approach Him (Psa. 65:2-5). In Psalm 65:5-13, David views creation as being the result of God's original supernatural action and maintained through His constant action. Thus, David sees the world around him as being directly influenced everyday by the creative power of God. David's thoughts of the supernatural leave no need for natural explanations.

Psalm 70

David experiences derealization in Psalm 70:1 and 70:5 as he thinks of God rushing to his side to deliver him from his enemies. Although David is facing a physical problem resulting from his enemies, he looks for a supernatural solution. In Psalm 70:4, David teaches his listeners to view God in a similar way. He encourages them to look to God for saving help, and to rejoice as they wait for God's deliverance. Thus, David encourages people to willingly take upon themselves derealization as a part of their religion.

Psalm 72

Psalm 72 is the last chronological psalm of David (Psa. 72:20). It was written in his final days after he selected Solomon as his successor.

David experiences depersonalization in Psalm 72:5-11 and 72:17 as he blesses his son, Solomon. Although David is addressing Solomon, David's mind sees glimpses of the future Messiah. This psalm describes the future reign of the Messiah in the lineage of David who would rule as long as the sun and moon. This future Messiah will be served by all nations (Psa. 72:11). And in His name all people would be blessed (Psa. 72:17).

Psalm 95

Although Psalm 95 contains no authorship information, Hebrews 4:7 tells us David authored it. David experiences derealization in Psalm 95:2-7—"seeing" God as the exalted King presiding over creation.

David experiences depersonalization as he associates his royal position with the supernatural God. Just as David became the king over the many nations he defeated, so he views God as supreme among other gods (Psa. 95:3). Within this depersonalization vision, God speaks and David captures His message in Psalm 95:7-11. God's message is intended to teach people so they do not harden their hearts against Him.

Psalm 103

David experiences depersonalization in Psalm 103:1-5 as he interacts with his own soul. Thus, David addresses himself as if he is another person. In this depersonalization, David encourages his own soul to praise God and look to Him as the source of blessing, forgiveness, love, and youthful vigor.

David experiences derealization in Psalm 103:6-22 as he "sees" the Lord interacting with humanity. David explains that God cares for the oppressed (Psa. 103:6). David points to the Law of Moses as God's revelation to humanity (Psa. 103:7, 18). He notes God is compassionate and will not remain angry forever (Psa. 103:8-11). This compassion leads God to provide complete redemption for His children (Psa. 103:12-13).

David concludes this psalm with a depersonalization vision where he associates his own throne room experience with the Lord upon His throne (Psa. 103:19-22). Just as David had servants and mighty men to do his bidding; the Lord God has mighty angels to carry out His will.

Psalm 122

In Psalm 122:1-4, David provides encouragement to future generations who will worship in Jerusalem. He leads the people in spiritual prayer for the peace, security and prosperity of Jerusalem for the sake of the Lord's house (Psa. 122:6-9). In this psalm, David experiences depersonalization as he reflects on God dwelling in His house just as David dwells in his house (Psa. 122:1, 5, 9).

Psalm 131

In Psalm 131:1-2, David teaches humility, quietness of spirit and contentment. He points to his hope in the Lord as the source of this personal peace (Psa. 131:3). When considering the numerous, incredibly traumatic experiences of David, it is amazing his faith allowed him to experience such calmness and contentment. Although this is a short psalm, it is stunningly powerful when we consider the warrior who penned it. Thus, the warrior recaptures the shepherd of his past.

Psalm 133

In Psalm 133:1, David teaches unity for the people of God. David uses the metaphor of the anointing oil for unity. This is a fitting picture of unity, as the Holy Spirit rests upon the anointed and is Himself the source of unity among the faithful. Just as the oil spreads and finds itself everywhere upon the anointed, the Holy Spirit also moves unhindered in the lives of all those who trust in the Lord (Psa. 133:2 & John 3:8).

David experiences derealization in Psalm 133:3. In this verse, David "sees" God commanding his blessing to remain upon Mount Zion forever. Within this vision is contained a snapshot of eternity.

Psalm 145

David experiences depersonalization in Psalm 145:1-2 as he "sees" a glimpse of God's splendor through reflecting on his own circumstances as king. God is called "King" and He is the subject of eternal praise upon His throne.

David experiences derealization in Psalm 145:3-20 as he "sees" God presiding over endless generations of humanity (Psa. 145:4-7, 16, 20). David describes God as loving and slow to anger (Psa. 145:8). God cares for those who fall and the downcast people within society, but promises to destroy the wicked (Psa. 145:14, 20). And whenever a person calls upon the Lord, He is always faithful to answer (Psa. 145:18-19).

David teaching us to "See" as He "Sees"

Whereas in the examination of the "Experience Psalms" and "Symptom Psalms" we see David's imagination working overtime to "see" plots, death threats, danger and flashbacks; here in the "Seeing Psalms" we see David's mind working to "see" God everywhere. This is a major blessing to David, and shows us that although the symptoms of PTSD can be devastating, there is hope found within them. David was not abandoned to hopelessness. Rather, his PTSD disability later allowed him to clearly "see" God.

Without his PTSD it is likely David would have never "seen" God. Therefore, the development of PTSD within David is likely the most beneficial contributor to David's spirituality. Without PTSD, David would have never had occasion to pen the psalms as he would not have a traumatic driving force compelling him to constant prayer.

Although the Seeing Psalms are inspiring, they also serve to demonstrate David's severe misunderstanding of people as a result of his PTSD social impairment. David supposes here that others can also "see" God as he "sees" Him. Frankly, they cannot. For a person to develop a similar capability to "see" God, they must either endure trauma, or take great care to develop this skill through learning from trauma survivors like David.

In the Seeing Psalms, David supposes the faithful can "see" God's acts, splendor, glory and works, and this "vision" compels them to tell others (Psa. 145:10-12, 15). In this David is showing his deep misunderstanding of others—as these people likely lacked the PTSD depersonalization symptom which allowed David to "see" God. Here David assumes that the people who believe in society can also "see" as he "sees." Although this is a small point, it may serve elsewhere to further David's social impairment in the Experience Psalms and Symptom Psalms. David assumes others can "see" as he "sees."

Due to his PTSD, David is different than normal citizens, so his assumption may have led to frustration and further feelings of isolation at various times as he later found other believers viewed God differently from him. By sharing his view of God with others, David made it possible for common people to learn how to use derealization and depersonalization in their own spirituality. Thus, David's psalms radically transformed Bible spirituality.

We must transform "Reality" to "See" God

The Seeing Psalms provide teachings through David's PTSD derealization and depersonalization (Psa. 15, 24, 29, 65, 70, 72, 95, 103, 122, 131, 133 and 145). Overall, the Seeing Psalms show us how to "see" God in the way David "saw" Him. Within these psalms, all the negative PTSD symptoms have been removed. Although devastating throughout his life, we see here the good product of that trauma. David's method of "seeing" God is a proven means of overcoming tragedy. By learning to "see" God in the same way as David, a believer is able to gain a similar ability to persevere in the midst of trauma.

Today we should view derealization and depersonalization as inseparable parts of the Christian faith. It is possible to teach the Bible without using these techniques. However, any appeal to God's activity in the natural world is by definition "seeing" the supernatural within the natural world. By essence this is derealization.

So, by necessity, for a person to believe in the supernatural world of the Bible, that person must change their definition of "reality." A Bible believer holds there are supernatural events which occur beyond the ability of our eyes to perceive them. Bible faith requires believers to use a type of derealization—a symptom of PTSD which occurs as the affected mind perceives supernatural (beyond natural) events in order to cope with trauma.

Moreover, messianic prophecy throughout the Bible adopts David's method of depersonalization. From David forward, the prophecies which describe the Messiah focus on "seeing" Him. This is only possible through future prophet experiencing depersonalization similar to what was shown in David's messianic prophecies.

172

In other words, Biblical faith was developed through the PTSD of David. God spoke to David and all future prophets through the PTSD lens of David. Therefore, we can understand the development of Biblical faith by carefully examining the traumatic experiences and subsequent PTSD of David. Trauma is the gateway through which we can gain an understanding of the historical formation of Bible faith. When we understand trauma, faith is no longer derided as a mere delusion or imagination.

Trauma establishes faith as practical and necessary. Faith is the means through which ancient people survived repeated trauma. It is no wonder why all surviving ancient human societies were religious. Faith is the means through which humans make sense of tragedy and find the strength to "survive." History demonstrates human societies are incapable of surviving long-term without faith. Faith is the only way people survived.

Section 4: How David Transformed Bible Faith by Influencing Future Believers to "See" God

As previously discussed, David transformed messianic prophecy in the Bible through the PTSD symptom depersonalization. Before David, messianic prophecies focused on impersonal traits of Christ. Whereas, after David, messianic prophecies focus on personal visions of the Christ actually experienced by the prophets. Thus, in the Bible, prophets after David adopt his pattern of depersonalization.

Prophecies of the Messiah are not only written by the prophets, but the prophets experience for themselves the feelings of the Christ—being spiritually transported to future events. In this section we will compare the messianic prophecies of the Bible which occur before and after David. It will become clear David's PTSD was instrumental in the development of Bible prophecy. His PTSD serves as the lens through which all future prophets see future events.

Comparison of Messianic Prophecies before and after David
How David's PTSD Depersonalization Influenced Future Bible Prophets

Before David: Messianic Prophecies Focus on *Impersonal Traits* of Messiah

Before David, there were some messianic prophecies spoken directly by the Lord Himself, and there are others which were spoken by human prophets. Our goal is to determine how *human* prophets viewed God, so we will briefly discuss and dismiss the prophecies delivered by the Lord Himself before we solely consider the prophecies delivered by human prophets.

Prophecies Spoken by the Lord Himself
In Genesis 3:15, it states the seed of the woman would crush the serpent's head. This prophecy was directly spoken by the Lord Himself. As such this prophecy is not helpful to this discussion because it is a picture of how the Lord sees Himself; not how the Lord is viewed by a human prophet.

In Genesis 12:3 and 22:18, the Lord tells Abraham he will be the source of blessing to all peoples. This ultimate source of blessing is the Messiah who would be a descendant of Abraham. A similar occurrence is found in Genesis 17:19 and 21:12 as the Lord Himself indicates the Messiah lineage would be through Isaac. However, due to these prophecies being spoken by the Lord Himself, they are outside the scope of this discussion similar to Genesis 3:15.

In Exodus 12:46, the Lord Himself describes the Passover lamb—stating that none of its bones can be broken. This is messianic as it offers a description of the future Messiah whose legs would not be broken upon the cross. However, similar to Genesis 3:15; 12:3; 17:19; 21:12; 22:18, this prophecy is outside the scope of our discussion due to this prophecy being spoken by the Lord Himself. (Even if permitted in our discussion here, all of the above prophecies still describe only "impersonal traits" of the

Messiah, simply identifying His human lineage without the "personal vision" aspect which characterizes messianic prophecies after David.)

So apart from the prophecies directly spoken by the Lord Himself above, let's discuss the human-delivered prophecies below to determine how human prophets viewed the Messiah before David . . .

Prophecies Spoken by Human Prophets

In Genesis 49:10, Jacob prophecies of the Messiah who would be born in the clan of Judah. Jacob states that the Messiah would rule over nations.

In Deuteronomy 18:15, the author describes the Messiah as a future prophet like Moses.

In Numbers 24:17, Balaam saw a far off vision of the Messiah who would later rule over nations.

In these three prophecies, delivered by Jacob, Moses and Balaam, we are offered descriptions of "impersonal traits" of the Messiah. Jacob tells of a future ruler in the house of Judah. Moses speaks of another prophet like himself. Last, Balaam states he sees a "far off" vision of an Israelite ruler.

In all three prophecies, we find something dramatically different than the descriptions of the Lord by David. When David described the Lord, we see something remarkably personal and present. David did not describe the Lord as someone who is "far off," but rather as a present refuge/fortress/stronghold/rock/deliverer. David did not see the majesty of the Lord from a distance. Rather, David experienced the majesty of the Lord everywhere around him. He saw God as being present in maintaining creation, in granting him victory in battle, and in overseeing all the actions of humanity from His heavenly throne.

Moving forward from David, the prophets after David adopted his method of prophecy. This is why the prophets after David began to describe the Messiah as if they were standing next to Him, or even experiencing events from within His body. There would be no more impersonal prophecies of the Lord as if far away (Num. 24:17). Instead, when describing the Messiah, the future prophets would be transported within His presence similar to how the PTSD depersonalization of David allowed him to achieve this. In this way, the PTSD of David dramatically transformed and influenced how all future prophets would relate to God.

After David: Messianic Prophecies Focus on *Personal Visions* of Messiah

It is possible that some of the prophets after David experienced a disability similar to David's PTSD, which led to them developing depersonalization as an independent symptom of their own disabilities. Another possibility is that future prophets merely incorporated the PTSD symptom of David into their own spirituality—essentially teaching themselves to view the Lord similar to how David viewed the Lord. Whatever the cause, it is clear the PTSD of David marked a permanent change in how future generations would "see" and relate to God.

Below I will discuss various messianic prophecies which occur after David. Also, I will also discuss passages from 2 Samuel and other Psalm authors which were likely influenced by David's depersonalization method. The prophecies below will demonstrate the depersonalization method of David was used by future prophets.

In 2 Samuel 7:12-13, the prophet Nathan offers a depersonalization of the David's son—declaring his kingdom would endure forever. Whereas Solomon would build the house of the Lord; the future Messiah as the son of David would endure forever (2 Sam. 7:13).

In Psalm 45:6-7, a son of Korah experiences depersonalization as recites his verses for the king (Psa. 45:1). As the son of Korah views the human king, his mind shifts to a vision of the heavenly King, the Lord God, who would reign forever (Psa. 45:6).

In Psalm 78:2, Asaph experiences depersonalization as he sees the world through the eyes of the Messiah—declaring He will speak in parables to declare things from ancient times. Thus, Asaph's feelings are conflated with the actual experience of the future Messiah. Asaph "feels" in that moment what the Messiah would later feel.

In Psalm 80:17-19, Asaph "sees" the Lord God providing restoration for the people through the son of man whom He raises up at His right hand. Asaph experiences depersonalization through this vision as he is transported within the heavenly throne room. At first, Asaph asks God to look down from heaven (Psa. 80:14). But once Asaph receives a glimpse of God's throne, he calls God's attention to the redeeming "son of man" who is at His right hand (Psa. 80:17). Asaph does not relate to God impersonally, but rather interacts with Him based on what he sees within the court of heaven.

In Psalm 89:3-36, Ethan the Ezrahite experiences depersonalization as he reflects on God's relationship with David. Throughout this psalm, the vision of Ethan captures thoughts of the human kings within David's lineage, while simultaneously capturing visions of the Messiah king who would reign forever (Psa. 89:3-4, 29, 36-37).

In Psalm 107:28-30, an anonymous author experiences depersonalization in his future vision of the circumstances of people at the arrival of the Messiah. Specifically, the author details how the Messiah would be on a ship where the people were distressed during a storm. The Lord delivers them from tempest as He calms the waves and guides them to their haven.

In Psalm 118:22-27, an anonymous author experiences depersonalization in his future vision of the Messiah. Specifically, the author details how the Messiah would be the rejected cornerstone who would arrive in the Name of the Lord. He describes events as if he is present.

In Hosea 11:1, the prophet experiences depersonalization as he speaks for God. Therefore the prophet is ushered into a vision where he experiences what God Himself experiences in calling for the Messiah to come forth from Egypt.

In Isaiah 6:9-10, the prophet Isaiah is transported into the heavenly throne room. He experiences depersonalization through this "out of body" experience where he captures a distinct reality of the Messiah's earthly ministry: Although the people would hear the words of the Messiah, they would refuse to understand Him.

179

In Isaiah 7:14, the prophet receives a vision of the future Messiah's virgin birth. Isaiah experiences depersonalization as the prophecy was fulfilled both in his own time and also in the distant future (Isa. 8:3-4). Thus the fulfillment is obscured through both Isaiah's son and the later Messiah. Although this prophecy was fulfilled partially with Isaiah, it also was not completed with him. Thus, it was both something he experienced and also something he did not experience.

In Isaiah 9:1-2, Isaiah experiences depersonalization as he sees the Messiah's light blazing over the horizon upon those people held captive in darkness. Isaiah describes the experience as if he is present (Isa 9:2).

In Isaiah 9:6-7, the prophet sees the eternal kingdom of the Messiah—declaring incredible paradox later realized in Christ. Although the Messiah would be a child, He would also have an eternal kingdom. If a person were simply speaking of what they knew, such a paradox would be something they would refuse writing. If however the person experienced it, no matter how paradoxical, they would maintain that somehow it must be made true—even if it does not make sense at first. This is the nature of this depersonalization of Isaiah in this passage. Although seemingly impossible, he still saw it. This stunning paradox is later made reality.

In Isaiah 11:1-4, the prophet experiences depersonalization as he "sees" the exaltation of the future Messiah who is born through the lineage of Jesse. Isaiah sees the righteous judgment of the Messiah as He governs all people with equity.

In Isaiah 40:3-5, Isaiah sees the arrival of John the Baptist—who cultivates the hearts of the people in preparation for the Messiah. He experiences depersonalization as he witnesses these events for himself.

In Isaiah 50:6, the prophet experiences depersonalization as he feels for himself the flogging endured by the Lord Jesus.

In Isaiah 52:13-53:12, Isaiah experiences depersonalization as he "sees" the Messiah enduring his trial, crucifixion, burial, resurrection and the eternal redemption it purchased for those who believe.

In Isaiah 61:1-2, the prophet experiences depersonalization as he feels for himself the experience of the future Messiah. Isaiah speaks for the

Messiah—declaring he has this same mission. Whereas in other passages, Isaiah speaks for the Lord; here Isaiah speaks for the Messiah.

In Jeremiah 31:15, the prophet Jeremiah experiences depersonalization as he hears weeping at the loss of children in Ramah. Here the Lord tells Jeremiah about the weeping.

In Micah 5:2, the prophet Micah experiences depersonalization as he speaks for the Lord to call forth the Messiah ruler from Bethlehem.

In Daniel 2:44, the prophet Daniel views the future, eternal kingdom of the Messiah through the vision of Nebuchadnezzar. Through depersonalization, Daniel "sees" the future and also "sees" the dream of the king.

In Daniel 7:13-14, the prophet "sees" for himself a heavenly vision where the son of man is led into the presence of the Ancient of Days. Daniel experiences depersonalization as he has this "out of body" vision.

In Zechariah 9:9, the prophet Zechariah "sees" and shouts out for others to "see" the Messiah. He experiences depersonalization as he witnesses the arrival of the Messiah upon a donkey.

In Zechariah 11:12-13, Zechariah experiences depersonalization as he is transported within Judas to "see" the betrayal of the Messiah firsthand. Zechariah likely felt the weight of the coins as they were dropped into his hand. Thus, this is not a poetic description, but a spiritual transportation to the event as it occurred in future history.

In Zechariah 12:10, the prophet experiences depersonalization as he speaks for the Messiah who was rejected. He also experiences for himself the inward grief of the people as they repent.

In Malachi 4:5-6, the prophet Malachi experiences depersonalization as he speaks for the Lord—who promises to precede the arrival of Messiah with another prophet. This was fulfilled with John the Baptist.

Before David, messianic prophecy related only impersonal traits of the Messiah—specifically that He would be a ruler born of woman, in the lineage of Abraham, Isaac, Jacob and Judah (Gen. 3:15; 12:3; 17:19; 21:12; 22:18; 49:10; Exo. 12:46; Deu. 18:15; Num. 24:17). David transformed messianic prophecy by teaching people they could experience God's presence for themselves.

After David, prophets actually experience by "seeing" for themselves events during the Messiah's earthly ministry (2 Sam. 7:12-13; Psa. 45:6-7; 78:2; 80:17-19; 89:3-36; 107:28-30; 118:22-27; Hos. 11:1; Isa. 6:9-10; 7:14; 9:1-7; 11:1-4; 40:3-5; 50:6; 52:13-53:12; 61:1-2; Jer. 31:15; Mic. 5:2; Dan. 2:44; 7:13-14; Zech. 9:9; 11:12-13; 12:10; Mal. 4:5-6). This is a result of the prophets using the "PTSD depersonalization" method of David—either as a symptom of a psychological disability they developed, or by them merely incorporating the elements of David's spiritual writing.

How David's PTSD Derealization Influenced Bible Faith and Believers

"Seeing" God after David

The derealization symptom of David's PTSD led him to develop a view of God which was remarkably present and helpful in all areas of his life. David viewed God as being at work in the world around him—sustaining creation, blessing and punishing people and protecting the faithful from harm. In the ancient world, this concept of God was especially useful in equipping people to deal with the traumatic experiences they would face.

Although humans will indeed experience trauma, the faith of David provides a means for the individual to "survive." Therefore, the faith of David is centered upon survival. No matter how difficult the trauma one faces, David teaches us it can be survived through one's direct relationship with God.

A person can learn to "see" God at work around them even when the world appears chaotic. A person can choose to "see" divine order which gives meaning in the midst of mayhem. Even when surrounded by danger, in an inescapable situation, a person can choose to "see" the fortress of God surrounding and protecting them supernaturally. This is the faith of David.

How David Transformed Faith in the Bible

To simplify Old Testament history, the period of time from Moses to David is about as long as the period of time from David to the restoration from exile. Both of these periods are about 400-500 years each. So how does the spirituality of each period compare with one another?

Following Moses, there is a decline in how the faith was perceived and practiced by the common people. The conquest commanded through Moses was abandoned (Judg. 1:27-2:3). Ultimately the people abandoned the commands of Moses as everyone did as they saw fit (Judg. 21:25). There were some faithful people who remained, however their view of God was a much lesser view than the robust faith of Moses. From time to time a

183

faithful man or woman would arise as a judge over Israel, but the people waned and lacked unifying leadership (Judg. 2:18-19).

However, the faith of the Bible is rejuvenated with the life of David. Although there were kings who were unrighteous throughout the history of Israel and Judah, the people were unified in the derealization faith of David. There were so many prophets that there were even schools to train them (2 Kings 2:15 & 4:38). Prophets began to "see" many visions of present and future events—recording them as if they were experiencing the events firsthand. This Old Testament pattern can be traced to David's derealization and his view of God as present, personal and helpful to individuals.

In essence, David allowed the people to "see" God near them. God was no longer viewed upon the inapproachable mountain of Moses. Rather, God was viewed by David as transporting that incredible glory to normal people—to protect them in the midst of daily trauma. This new view of faith was inspiring to common people as it invited each person to experience God firsthand. Thus, the PTSD of David caused a dramatic shift in his view of God, which inspired countless others to adopt a derealization view of God.

Trauma is the gateway to spiritual faith. Understanding trauma is the gateway to understanding spiritual faith. God allowed Biblical faith to be formed through the PTSD of David. The faith of David challenges people to change their perception of what they consider to be "real." God can be experienced. One needs to learn to look beyond the natural curtain to "see" the supernatural actions of God. Thus, David's PTSD allows him to teach future generations to walk by faith, not by sight.

How Believers Today can use Derealization

The Bible encourages all people to "adopt" derealization in order to experience the unseen, supernatural presence of God. In other words, David suffered the trauma and the other symptoms of PTSD, but he only "passes on" the useful "symptoms" to those who would follow in his spiritual footsteps. As a result, derealization becomes a permanent part of Biblical faith—having been first learned by those who survived trauma. Biblical faith is a PTSD symptom which is willingly accepted by those who choose to believe. It is the means through which the faithful "learn" to "see" God at work in the world around them.

The Bible tells us about people who faced incredible trauma in the ancient world. The Bible is a series of stories which tell us about those people who survived horrific experiences. The Bible teaches us about a faith that can persevere through the most difficult experiences imaginable. If a person chooses to adopt the derealization of David, they now possess a time-tested, proven ability to face the biggest giants. Thus, the PTSD of David teaches us the essence of Biblical faith: We can "see" the unseen. We can find inexhaustible courage and strength in the fortress of the Lord. We can "see" the Lord interacting with the world around us.

This substitutionary pattern is reflected in the work of Christ. David experienced trauma, but passed on only the positive result of trauma to those who followed him in the faith. Similarly, Christ experienced the trauma of the cross, but passed on only the positive result of trauma to those who follow Him. Thus to deny David the full recognition of the trauma he endured and survived is akin to denying Christ of the trauma He endured.

As was the case with the Good Shepherd, His under-shepherds were appointed to endure trauma for the betterment of those who would follow. David lived and died to teach us derealization. Christ lived and died to provide the final benefit to all who have adopted the Biblical derealization of David. The unseen refuge of David is physically realized through the work of Christ (John 14:3).

Indeed, the kingdom of heaven is near—just as the Lord Jesus told us. This heavenly kingdom is the same refuge/fortress/stronghold which

David spiritually "saw" around him—protecting him and strengthening him for battle. Likewise, today the kingdom of heaven does not arrive with our careful observation. Rather the kingdom of heaven is something we view with the inward vision of our spirits. We are ever in the midst of this kingdom of heaven. It is as close as we desire it to be—providing for us a direct link from our battlefields to the throne room of God in the highest heaven.

Believers Change their Perception of "Reality" to "See" God

In Ezekiel 1, we are offered a stunning picture of the Glory of God, which appears as an awesome wheeled machine with various angels and the presence of the Lord atop it all. While in exile, after experiencing the trauma of separation, Ezekiel's mind was reeling to make sense of his experiences. However, in the midst of his trauma, Ezekiel's eyes were opened. He saw that, above the world of humanity, God's kingdom was an incredibly complex machine, being governed by angels and directed by the Lord Himself. This provided comfort to Ezekiel: Although Ezekiel could not make sense of the world, God was directing the movement of powerful supernatural machines to transform it.

When facing trauma, especially repeated and inescapable trauma, the individual has two choices: (1) fall apart under the pressure or (2) survive. Faith allows a person to "survive" by allowing them to change their perception of reality . . .

If they see injustices in the world, they can choose to "see" God preparing to judge the world in righteousness (Psa. 145:3-20).

If a person needs help, they can be confident God hears their prayers (Psa. 65:2-5).

If a person is scared, they can choose to "see" angels protecting them (2 Kings 6:17).

If a person is trapped on a battlefield or in a foreign territory, they can choose to "see" the supernatural fortress of God which protects them from above (Ezek. 1:1-28).

186

If a person feels alone, abandoned, betrayed or imprisoned, they can choose to "see" God standing at their side (Psa. 16:8).

A person of faith chooses to change their perception of "reality" to accommodate the supernatural God and His kingdom (Matt. 4:17 & Luke 17:20-21). This supernatural perception is a requirement of Bible faith. Moreover, it provides a powerful means of survival for the faithful— allowing them to face trauma with the same method used by David to "survive" countless battlefields.

Like Ezekiel, the believer today can choose to "see" God's powerful kingdom moving above them. It is like an inexhaustible battery which provides an endless source of strength, courage, gifts, talents and abilities to those who draw from its mighty supernatural wheels.

And when considering this supernatural kingdom is near to us all, our perception of God's greatness is increased. God's Spirit is not a single fortress. Rather, God's kingdom can be "seen" above every believer simultaneously throughout the earth. So, when our spiritual eyes are opened we are able to see above us, everywhere and in every direction, the great angelic machines in the sky which follow and protect each believer. From this omnipresent network of angelic machines, God sustains all biological life on earth (Psa. 104:27-30). Since God sustains even the smallest creatures of earth, we can be confident in our supernatural faith that He will sustain us always—even in the midst of the most difficult trauma (Matt. 6:26).

Section 5: Final Reflections

As in the case with theology, many things are debated. I have spent much time praying and considering my thoughts within this book. And, as in the case of all good discussions, I have considered the strengths and limitations of my own work. Below I will leave you with my thoughts on how I evaluate my own work. Perhaps this can be helpful for you as you consider your own thoughts on this topic.

Strengths of My Book

In preparing this book, I have reflected on the reasons why some people believe the Bible and others do not. My goal here is to present faith in a way that can provide consensus and mutual ground. Although people may not believe in God's existence, I am confident my book shows why people have faith and why it is very useful.

Perhaps this book can provide a good starting point for discussion: Trauma is the foundation of human faith. I am confident this topic can serve as a catalyst for useful discussion—regardless of the starting point from which we each approach the Bible. This discussion may open our understanding to many things in human history which were previously out of reach.

Faith and Surviving

Faith is about surviving. Simply put, David survived. Faith is the means through which David survived trauma in the ancient world we likely cannot fathom. Within my perspective, I view PTSD as the natural response of David's mind to repeated trauma. And within those PTSD symptoms, God "spoke" to David—giving him strength and courage to continue living in the midst of impossible odds.

As we begin to understand more about trauma, we further establish the subjective, personal effect of faith in the individual. Perhaps in our world we get it all wrong. Many objective arguments have been offered in

189

an attempt to either prove or disprove "God's existence." I submit the perspective that this debate is wholly irrelevant to the faithful.

Faith is about subjective, personal coping—it is not about trying to prove objective existence of God to a skeptic. The point of the Bible is to tell people they have everlasting hope and a means to survive trauma through belief. The point is not to establish "objective" points in order to coerce someone to agree to something. So, by divorcing faith from its roots in trauma, many err today in their apologetics. David did not set out to "prove" God to others, but to simply share how his faith helped him to endure and can help others to endure. Today, the faith of David beckons us to return to the roots of Biblical faith . . . the survival of trauma.

I am a former U.S. Marine. When deploying to war, my wife gave me a simple command: *"Come home to us. No matter what, come home to us."*

We had candid discussions with family about the possibility of injury and all the things which war could "do" to me. We framed our expectations with an honest consideration of incredible trauma. But no matter what, my wife's command on future deployments was always the same . . . *"No matter what, come home to us."*

After "surviving" and continuing to survive, experience after experience, day after day, I can say I understand the purpose of faith as a "survival mechanism." When everything is chaotic, it is so powerful to think of God organizing all the pieces to make them come together. The mighty fortress of Ezekiel 1 demonstrates that even when things are completely lost and out of control, the wheels of God's supernatural machines are still moving—generating power for the faithful.

Anyone who has survived trauma and loss understands this. When we experience loss, often things do not make sense. We search for meaning in a person's last words, our last interactions, why this happened, what could have been done to prevent this, and so on.

Our human minds are always searching to make sense of the world around us. Our minds are so adept at recognizing faces, that when we see leaves in a tree our subconscious minds can trace out eyes, a nose and a mouth. If we enter a dark room, our eyes may imagine seeing things. If we hear radio static, our minds subconsciously work overtime to try to identify "words" within it.

So faith indeed is an inseparable part of being human. We want to make sense of the seemingly chaotic world around us. Although *"confirmation bias,"* the *"placebo effect,"* and *"false positives"* can muddy the waters, even the most skeptical should concede to the power contained within faith—that it helps struggling people survive. It is logical when we are presented with trauma, our subconscious minds will do everything to try to make sense of it—to the point we can think of it all being controlled by God. This is an interesting topic that should be explored fully to understand our ancient human ancestors. This will serve as a pathway to self-understanding.

Therefore, faith should not be derided or dismissed. Hope is a part of the human experience. It does not need to be proven as part of an "objective" fact. We should not seek to dishonor the subjective, personal power of God by relegating Him to a debatable point that should be "objectively" proven to the skeptic.

In years past, at some point, people developed the view that God's existence must be "objectively" proven or disproven. I put forward the thought that this may be due to the comforts of the modern world. People have become so accustomed to ease that they have forgotten the common trauma that daily held captive our ancient ancestors. And, as such, with a lessened understanding of the common human experience, people today venture to place "God" within an experiment to determine His existence. This is a mistake and demonstrates we may have shifted altogether from the original foundation of faith itself as a survival mechanism. In other words, humans have lost touch with what it means to be "human."

When faith is understood as a subjective survival mechanism, all that matters is whether it "works." As long as it helps the person survive, it is "true" in its incredibly valuable purpose. The writers of the Bible were not concerned with laying out objective proofs of God's existence. Either people chose to "believe" as a subjective, personal act or they did not.

The Invisible Scaffolding

Imagine a person deserted on an island. After many days of tireless work, he finally scrapes together what he needs to survive. He found fresh water and coconuts to sustain himself, and a great tree under which he finds shelter from the heat of the day.

Then, without warning, the island is devastated by a powerful storm. While sheltering under the great tree, it snaps and falls before the storm subsides.

In the aftermath of this disaster, the forest floor is littered with all the items which once composed the island—trees and plants. Now bereft of shelter, the man must rebuild something to give him respite from the scorching sun and future storms.

As he struggles with the decision of what he should do, his eye glimpses what appears to be writing on the trunk of the giant tree. . . .

"Go to the northernmost point of the island. There is an invisible, unmovable scaffolding built upon the rock. Build upon it. If it remains unused, it will soon vanish."

It looks as if the giant tree shattered to reveal this writing which was always contained within. Although the writing appears on the stump, outlines of the words appear scorched in reverse on the base of the fallen tree.

Having no other good options, the person sets out to find the rock at the northernmost point of the island. Upon arriving, he carefully approaches with his hands extended to grasp the invisible beams he believes he will find. Once he finds the beams, he places mud upon them so he can see the outer edges upon which he must build.

The man begins picking up the rubble left in the wake of the powerful storm. First, he approaches the invisible scaffolding with a shattered tree branch in hand. Thinking he may have to lean the branch upon the invisible scaffolding, he places it on the ground with one end touching the muddy beam.

Yet to his surprise, when the branch touches the beam, it "locks" into place. When he attempts to jostle it loose, the branch resists. It seems as if the branch is somehow "sticking" to the invisible beam.

The man then returns with another fragment left behind by the storm. This time, he takes a tree branch and pushes it on the beam horizontally above the ground. When pushing the shattered branch upon the beam, it clicks, locking into place. Remarkably it seems the invisible beam was somehow created to fit this *exact* branch in this *exact* position. As predicted, the branch sticks—and now appears suspended in the air.

Being greatly encouraged by this discovery, the man moves frantically to benefit fully from this invisible scaffolding. All the island rubble he carries back to the rock finds a *perfect* place in the emerging house—granting a visible structure for the roof, walls and floor. The otherwise invisible scaffolding becomes a visible reality for the man. In the following days, he now has shelter from the scorching heat of the sun and threats of future storms.

In this example, it points out the subjective, personal relevance of faith in God. To the weathered, desperate man on the deserted island, the "invisible scaffolding" provided encouragement to him in the mystifying horror in the storm's aftermath. The scaffolding provided a structure upon which he could rebuild.

Moreover, the scaffolding makes perfect sense of all the rubble left behind by the storm. Rather than regarding those pieces as rubble, the scaffolding welcomes them—allowing all of these past evidences of the storm to be incorporated into a grand vision. The remnants of the storm now gain purpose. Remarkably, those same shattered pieces now become the roof and walls within which the man now finds safety. The man begins to be thankful for the storm which allowed him to find this new home.

Faith is about survival. To the person who survives, faith in God provides the means to rebuild and to actually assign purpose to the shattered pieces of the past. Thus, for those who have endured trauma, faith is a venture of relevance. To the desperate, life becomes an issue of survival.

The things which help become valuable as the person scrapes to survive each hour of every day in the midst of grief.

Now imagine a ship captain arriving at the deserted island. Upon his approach, he views the ramshackle outline of what appears to be a large house made entirely of rubble upon the northernmost rock of the island. The ship captain anchors his boat and comes ashore to meet the man within the "house."

After enduring such tragedy and building a home with the rubble of the past storm, could anything be said to the man to convince him that the "invisible scaffolding" was not *real*? Seeing the home, and how it helped the man to eke out a living upon this inhospitable island, would it be reasonable for the ship captain to critically examine the story of the house? Regardless, no matter what could be said, nothing could convince the man that the "invisible scaffolding" did not exist.

This is a picture of faith and trauma. When we understand how faith enabled the people of the Bible to survive the most horrific events, should we ever venture to question the validity of their faith? When seeing the outline of the ramshackle houses they built from the rubble of trauma, should we not be convinced? When the house is towering above the rock as a monument to the person's survival, do you still desire to peel back the rubble to see the "invisible beams?"

In the process of tearing back a layer of rubble, the ship captain commits a grave offense against the man who now holds every piece of the home as precious—as monuments to the past love extended to him by the Person who etched the note within the giant tree. Indeed, the man will rightly gasp and resist any effort the ship captain makes to assault the pieces of his home in pursuit of his irreverent knowledge. Either accept the validity of this towering home built of rubble, or do not. But the man will not permit the ship captain to visit any harm upon his home.

David and Disability—the Whole Person Concept

We might know more about David than any other person in the Bible. Not only do we have several books documenting his history, David also provided us with his prayers and thoughts in the Psalms. Nearly half of the psalms were written by David, offering us an unparalleled invitation into his mind. By examining his many psalms, we can determine what made David "tick."

As I studied this topic, I often wondered why David exhibited such large emotional swings in his psalms. When we view his psalms within the context of his traumatic experiences, all of the emotional shifts make perfect sense. David is a man who is struggling with PTSD. Remarkably, his psalms give us insight from the ancient world on how to survive despite intense hardships.

Rather than interacting with only a part of David, my book interacts with David as a "whole person." My book celebrates the weaknesses of David. He is welcomed, warmly—warts and all. When considering this dear man likely lived his entire life, never having someone truly understand him, I wanted to be the person to address him personally in my letters.

Many of us have disabilities, and it is helpful to consider the fact that David experienced PTSD as a lifelong disability. Rather than placing upon David the unreasonable expectation of perfection (as if he were a clean, well-dressed businessman), readers of the Bible should come to the sobering realization this man was in all ways traumatized by the horrors of life—as documented in the 26 Traumatic Experiences in Section 1. Do not deny David the opportunity to accept his past trauma and thus find healing. When referring to David, do so within the full context of the trauma this man survived.

Moreover, no one deserves to be shamed for their suffering. Rather, those who are struggling should be warmly invited to share their true feelings without the fear of stigma and judgment. So, if ever we are discussing David, we need to be most respectful and courteous. Indeed, he survived far more than could be endured by other men. And he did so as an act of sacrifice within history—to teach us the full dimensions of faith through derealization and depersonalization.

If we relate to David as a person with PTSD, then our understanding of the Psalms is imbued with wisdom. If, however, we deny David his humanity, rejecting the reality of his PTSD, we not only disrespect the man himself, but our entire understanding of the Bible suffers. In my book I speak directly to David because I want to provide encouragement to him in the midst of his suffering. The point is to honor this man who gave so much to teach others to walk closer with God. The goal is to express love to David in the midst of his emotional suffering.

God speaks through people with disabilities to provide encouragement to future generations. Although David suffered, God helped him through his suffering. If you are struggling with PTSD or a similar psychological disability, my hope is that you will be encouraged by my book. You can survive because David survived. God will not forsake you because He did not forsake David (Heb. 13:5).

Limitations of My Book

Account for Bias

When reading it is always necessary to account for the potential bias of the author. Although I have written this book under a pen name (Genesis Pilgrim), I want to provide you information about me. This will help you judge my thoughts accurately.

I served many years in the U.S. Marines, from rank Private (E-1) to First Sergeant (E-8). Honestly, I feel like I "barely survived"—spending many years where I was overextended and pressed beyond my limits, being compelled by love of country to give more and more.

Over time, experiences began to blur into one another, until all that remains is just a mess of unlabeled emotions and resulting apathy at the impossibility of arranging them due to memory loss. My experiences demonstrate to me the world indeed makes no sense—where nothing can be said to repair the damage of the past. For me, faith in God has been the only way through which I can pull all the pieces together and continue to survive.

Humans have always been "spiritual" creatures because it is the only way our minds can make sense of repeated and unceasing trauma. When pushed to our breaking point and beyond, humans "need" to have something non-physical to anchor themselves. It is the only way in which humans have successfully learned to cope with repeated trauma. Sure, modern society attempts to use medicine and therapy, but those things have limits. A human needs something that can sustain them supernaturally. This explains why all human societies in history had supernatural beliefs.

So, what would happen to humans if society completely abandoned belief in the "supernatural?" Frankly, I think this is an absolute impossibility as individuals will always be inclined, even on a genetic level, to desire to "believe" in something to help them. A society may become capable of insulating citizens against certain trauma, such as starvation or war, but eventually when bad times come humans will always revert back to faith as the historically proven method of trauma survival.

197

Errors

After proofreading this book several times, I am satisfied with it as published. Nevertheless, I am sure I may have overlooked several misspelled words and some other grammatical errors. I hope when you encounter these mistakes within the text, they will not distract you from understanding. I have done my best to eliminate grammatical errors in my writing, but I am not a professional editor. And, that is okay.

I have lived much of my life—ever chasing a standard of perfection. As a U.S. Marine, my uniforms always had to be "perfect." During my new life, however, I want to be flawed and less than perfect. I am not a perfect man. Likewise I am sure my book reflects my lack of perfection. In cases where you see flaws in my book, please use these errors to support the message: Just as David had flaws, so also my commentary on his life may be at times grammatically flawed. It is okay to be "human."

"Dear David" Letters

Writing the "Dear David" sections of this book have been therapeutic for me. At times I say to David some of the good things I have heard from past counselors. At other times I say the things I wish others would have said to me at different times in my life. Overall, I relate to him with respect in these letters—avoiding dragging him through the mud on his past actions. I challenge his false thoughts, direct him to help and provide encouragement to him which he might not receive from anyone else.

I think I have been equipped to write this book through my own suffering. Even though many things are difficult, my past experiences have shaped my understanding of how humans in past and present relate to trauma.

Many artists and enlightened individuals are not fully appreciated within their lifetimes. Realizing David may have experienced rejection and emotional separation from people for his entire lifetime, my heart broke for him. Since David loved me enough to pen his prayers for me, I wanted to return love by writing back to him. Surely, I love this warrior of the past, and overall I wanted to send back this love and appreciation to him—lifting him up in his struggles.

Perhaps you have more things you would write to David. Maybe I left out something you are convinced would have been especially helpful to him in a particular situation.

Today there are so many people who are suffering—carrying emotional burdens as they struggle to make sense of them. Although we cannot interact with David directly, we can be a positive influence in the lives of others.

Classification of Experience Psalms, Symptom Psalms and Seeing Psalms

In my writing I did my best to provide a classification system which would make sense of the emotional differences in David's psalms. I simplified all of his psalms into three types: Experience, Symptom and Seeing. The Experience Psalms contain elements I think can be convincingly traced to specific situations described in the books of Samuel. Whereas the Symptom Psalms do not contain elements which can be convincingly traced to specific situations. Last, the Seeing Psalms are the psalms which were intended by David to be used to help people "see" God for themselves. Therefore, the Seeing Psalms do not contain many of the PTSD symptoms, with the exception of derealization and depersonalization.

I think my classification system makes sense because it shows David originally experienced certain emotions linked to traumatic experiences (Experience Psalms). Then after David survived those traumatic experiences, his mind continued to be afflicted with PTSD symptoms (Symptom Psalms). Then David filters out all of the negativity, and intends to pass on the "positive" faith effects of derealization and depersonalization—enabling future generations to "see" God for themselves (Seeing Psalms).

Within this classification system, there are some psalms which could be classified as one type or another depending on the author's thoughts on details within each psalm. In some cases, I determined a psalm did not contain "convincing" enough evidence for me to assign it to a specific experience from 1 Samuel or 2 Samuel. In other cases you may think I went too far in assigning a certain psalm to a particular experience because you are not convinced by the details therein.

However, I think my classification system is sufficient in its thesis purpose: <u>Demonstrating David experienced PTSD linked to situations in his life (Experience Psalms), and after he mentally processed those emotions (Symptom Psalms), he made an intentional effort to pass on derealization and depersonalization to future generations as useful components of Bible faith—allowing each believer to "see" God for themselves (Seeing Psalms).</u> Overall, this classification system of David's psalms into these three types provides an adequate explanation of different emotional tones in the psalms.

Predictions

As a reasonable prediction, I would like to see people relate to faith within its remarkably traumatic context. From a natural perspective, the only reason for faith is to give people hope in the midst of physical tragedy. A person develops heart-felt faith as a survival mechanism—enabling them to endure situations their physical mind interprets as "impossible" otherwise.

From my perspective, it makes no sense to discuss "faith" without discussing its origin in "trauma." The people of the Bible were born into a remarkably violent world, and their faith was designed to help them survive it.

When understanding the norm of "trauma" in the ancient world, we see chaos indeed swallowed up all who do not find an effective way to establish themselves and fight back. Indeed, we could conclude there have existed all types of people at all times in the ancient world. But in the time of David and the earlier patriarchs, the only societies which survived contained the ones who learned to confront trauma and fight back.

When reading the Bible, we may feel inclined to object to its candid brutality—criticizing war and other ancient Near East cultural practices from our ethnocentric, privileged perspective. And in doing so, we can be convinced we would not have survived it. The story of David includes remarkably brutality which needs to be acknowledged within its context; not judged from a 21st century perspective.

Rather than avoiding discussions of brutality in the ancient world, those who venture to understand the Bible must acknowledge and interact with it within its cultural context. By doing so, we can finally "unlock" passages which have been utterly neglected by past generations of readers who abandoned the discussion of God as the One who subjectively "helps people survive" in favor of debates over "God's existence."

If one cannot respectfully and appropriately relate to passages like 1 Samuel 18:25-27 within their context, this may immediately demonstrate their cognitive dissonance with the integration of faith and trauma.

Moreover, if one cannot properly interact with human trauma in history, venturing to "objectively prove" the supernatural God with natural means will be a likewise fruitless journey. Explain human history before you venture to reach beyond it.

Too often it seems humans have forgotten suffering. When being brought back to the realization that life is fragile, we are soon thereafter ushered into the Presence of the supernatural. Think of trauma. Then we may "see" a glimpse of God.

If You Need Help

If you need help "surviving" through traumatic experiences in your past, let me encourage you to ask for help. A licensed counselor can become your ally. Do not feel as if you are alone. You have hope. The journey to recovery begins when you make the courageous decision to make a phone call or talk to your doctor.

Although a counselor cannot change past events, they can help you gain some relief from PTSD symptoms you experience. For example, "cognitive processing therapy" (CPT) can help you to trace each PTSD symptom to a specific cause—similar to how I have done with David in Sections 1 & 2 of this book.

After completing CPT for some of my war experiences, I have a better understanding of my PTSD symptoms. This allows me to address them better when they each pop up.

For me personally, it has been helpful speaking to counselors about my traumatic experiences in war. I have found each counselor has certain professional strengths. If I relate to each counselor based on their own merits, I can learn helpful things from each person.

Whereas society is inclined to view anyone who is differently abled as "disabled," the reality is "disabilities" often are "abilities" which can truly help the person and society as a whole. Although David had PTSD, it was his PTSD which created the social awkwardness that compelled him to focus on his relationship with God by writing his psalms. So, in David's case, he was "blessed" by his PTSD. Years later we are still being blessed by the words he penned in the midst of hardship.

When society tries to shame you for being differently abled, look at the things which make you different as strengths. Plus, what is the real benefit in being "like everyone else?" I hold dear the things which have made me different—even though those things have been traumatic. Our experiences set us apart. Although experiences can be traumatic, we can get help to somehow make sense of them—becoming stronger people through our past suffering.

Faith is about survival. You can survive. You can thrive. No matter what you have been through, you are never beyond God's reach. He will not give up on you.

God loves you and sent the Lord Jesus to die for you (John 3:16). David loves you and wrote his psalms to help you. I love you and I wrote this book to encourage you. There are other blessed, gifted counselors who love you and have spent years preparing to help *you*. You are not alone. Reach out for help. Keep fighting!

Survive.

Disclaimer: This book is not intended to diagnose readers with PTSD. If you, or anyone you know, is struggling with trauma, seek the advice of a licensed counselor. A licensed counselor can properly evaluate psychological disorders and provide a treatment plan, including cognitive processing therapy (CPT), to help you on the road to recovery.

Index #1

Bible Passages Referenced

Index #2

Post-Traumatic Stress Disorder (PTSD) Symptoms Referenced

Below is a condensed list of references to David's PTSD symptoms in my book. When looking up each reference, you can read each page to find behavioral clues in the text demonstrating how David exhibited the respective PTSD symptom.

Disclaimer: This book is not intended to diagnose readers with PTSD. If you, or anyone you know, is struggling with trauma, seek the advice of a licensed counselor. A licensed counselor can properly evaluate psychological disorders and provide a treatment plan, including cognitive processing therapy (CPT), to help you on the road to recovery.

Index #3: Detailed Table of Contents

Section 2: David's PTSD Symptoms & the Symptom Psalms
(Psalm 5, 6, 8, 11-14, 16, 19, 28, 36, 37, 39, 53, 62, 64, 68, 109, 110, 140, 141)

How David Fit PTSD Criteria
Direct Exposure to Trauma: Death, Threatened Death, Serious Injury, Violence
Witnessing Trauma: Death, Threatened Death, Serious Injury, Violence
Learning Relative/Close Friend Experienced Trauma: Death, Threatened Death, Serious Injury, Violence
Indirect Exposure in Course of Professional Duties (First Responders, Medics, Etc.)
Symptoms Not Due to Medication, Substance Abuse or Other Illness
Symptoms Persist After Trauma Long-Term

David's PTSD Symptoms
Avoidance of Trauma-Related Thoughts/Feelings
Avoidance of Trauma-Related External Reminders
Decreased Interest in Activities
Depersonalization
Derealization
Difficulty Concentrating
Difficulty Experiencing Positive Affect
Difficulty Sleeping
Emotional Distress
Exaggerated Blame of Self or Others for Causing the Trauma
Feeling Isolated
Flashbacks
Heightened Startle Reaction
Hypervigilance
Inability to Recall Key Features of the Trauma
Irritability or Aggression
Negative Affect
Nightmares
Overly Negative Assumptions about Oneself or the World
Physical Reactivity
Risky or Destructive Behavior
Social Impairment
Unwanted Upsetting Memories
Conclusion on the Symptom Psalms: Who is the "Fool" of David? (Psalm 14:3 & 53:1)

Section 3: David's PTSD Perception of Reality & the Seeing Psalms
(Psalm 15, 24, 29, 65, 70, 72, 95, 103, 122, 131, 133, 145)

Seeing Psalms Written During Periods of Isolation
Seeing Psalms Transform Faith through Derealization and Depersonalization
The Seeing Psalms
Psalm 15
Psalm 24
Psalm 29
Psalm 65
Psalm 70
Psalm 72
Psalm 95

Psalm 103
Psalm 122
Psalm 131
Psalm 133
Psalm 145
David teaching us to "See" as He "Sees"
We must transform "Reality" to "See" God

Section 4: How David Transformed Bible Faith by Influencing Future Believers to "See" God
Comparison of Messianic Prophecies before and after David
How David's PTSD Depersonalization Influenced Future Bible Prophets
Before David: Messianic Prophecies Focus on *Impersonal Traits* of Messiah
Prophecies Spoken by the Lord Himself
Prophecies Spoken by Human Prophets
After David: Messianic Prophecies Focus on *Personal Visions* of Messiah
How David's PTSD Derealization Influenced Bible Faith and Believers
"Seeing" God after David
How David Transformed Faith in the Bible
How Believers Today can use Derealization
Believers Change their Perception of "Reality" to "See" God

Section 5: Final Reflections
Strengths of My Book
Faith and Surviving
The Invisible Scaffolding
David and Disability—the Whole Person Concept
Limitations of My Book
Account for Bias
Errors
"Dear David" Letters
Classification of Experience Psalms, Symptom Psalms and Seeing Psalms
Predictions
If You Need Help